3D FACE PROCESSING
Modeling, Analysis and Synthesis

THE KLUWER INTERNATIONAL SERIES IN VIDEO COMPUTING

Series Editor

Mubarak Shah, Ph.D.

University of Central Florida
Orlando, USA

Other books in the series:

EXPLORATION OF VISUAL DATA
      Xiang Sean Zhou, Yong Rui, Thomas S. Huang ; ISBN: 1-4020-7569-3

VIDEO MINING
      Edited by Azriel Rosenfeld, David Doermann, Daniel DeMenthon;ISBN: 1-4020-7549-9

VIDEO REGISTRATION
      Edited by Mubarah Shah, Rakesh Kumar; ISBN: 1-4020-7460-3

MEDIA COMPUTING: COMPUTATIONAL MEDIA AESTHETICS
      Chitra Dorai and Svetha Venkatesh; ISBN: 1-4020-7102-7

ANALYZING VIDEO SEQUENCES OF MULTIPLE HUMANS: Tracking, Posture
Estimation and Behavior Recognition
      Jun Ohya, Akita Utsumi, and Junji Yanato; ISBN: 1-4020-7021-7

VISUAL EVENT DETECTION
      Niels Haering and Niels da Vitoria Lobo; ISBN: 0-7923-7436-3

FACE DETECTION AND GESTURE RECOGNITION FOR HUMAN-COMPUTER
INTERACTION
      Ming-Hsuan Yang and Narendra Ahuja; ISBN: 0-7923-7409-6

3D FACE PROCESSING
Modeling, Analysis and Synthesis

Zhen Wen

University of Illinois at Urbana-Champaign
Urbana, IL, U.S.A.

Thomas S. Huang

University of Illinois at Urbana-Champaign
Urbana, IL, U.S.A.

KLUWER ACADEMIC PUBLISHERS
Boston / Dordrecht / New York / London

Distributors for North, Central and South America:
Kluwer Academic Publishers
101 Philip Drive
Assinippi Park
Norwell, Massachusetts 02061 USA
Telephone (781) 871-6600
Fax (781) 681-9045
E-Mail: kluwer@wkap.com

Distributors for all other countries:
Kluwer Academic Publishers Group
Post Office Box 322
3300 AH Dordrecht, THE NETHERLANDS
Telephone 31 786 576 000
Fax 31 786 576 474
E-Mail: services@wkap.nl

   Electronic Services <http://www.wkap.nl>

Library of Congress Cataloging-in-Publication Data

Wen, Zhen.
   3D FACE PROCESSING: Modeling, Analysis and Synthesis / Zhen Wen,
   Thomas S. Huang
      p. cm.—(Kluwer international series in video computing)
   Includes bibliographical references and index.

   1. Computer vision. I. Huang, Thomas S. II. Title. III. Series.

ISBN 978-1-4419-5463-3 (PB)   e-ISBN 978-1-4020-8048-7

Contents

List of Figures

List of Tables

Preface

The advances in new information technology and media encourage deployment of multi-modal information systems with increasing ubiquity. These systems demand techniques for processing information beyond text, such as visual and audio information. Among the visual information human faces provide important cues of human activities. Thus they are useful for human-human communication, human-computer interaction (HCI) and intelligent video surveillance. 3D face processing techniques would enable (1) extracting information about the person's identity, motions and states from images of face in arbitrary poses; and (2) visualizing information using synthetic face animation for more natural human computer interaction. These aspects will help an intelligent information system interpret and deliver facial visual information, which is useful for effective interaction and automatic video surveillance.

In the last few decades, many interesting and promising approaches have been proposed to investigate various aspects of 3D face processing, although all these areas are still subject of active research. This book introduces the frontiers of 3D face processing techniques. It reviews existing 3D face processing techniques, including techniques for 3D face geometry modeling, 3D face motion modeling, 3D face motion tracking and animation. Then it discusses a unified framework for face modeling, analysis and synthesis. In this framework, we first describe techniques for modeling static 3D face geometry in Chapter 2. Next, in Chapter 3 we present our geometric facial motion model derived from motion capture data. Then we discuss the geometric-model-based 3D face tracking and animation in Chapter 4 and Chapter 5, respectively. Experimental results on very low bit-rate face video coding, real-time speech-driven animation are reported to demonstrate the efficacy of the geometric motion model. Because important appearance details are lost in the geometric motion model, we present a flexible appearance model in Chapter 6 to enhance the framework. We use efficient and effective methods to reduce the the appearance model's dependency on illumination and person. Then, in Chapter 7 and Chapter 8 we present experimental results to show the effectiveness of the flexible appearance model in face analysis and synthesis. In Chapter 9, we describe applications in which we apply the framework. Finally, we conclude this book with summary and comments on future work in 3D face processing framework.

ZHEN WEN AND THOMAS S. HUANG

Acknowledgments

We would like to thank numerous people who have helped with the process of writing this book. Particularly, we would like to thank the following people for discussions and collaborations which have influenced parts of the text: Dr. Pengyu Hong, Jilin Tu, Dr. Zicheng Liu and Dr. Zhengyou Zhang. We would thank Dr. Brian Guenter, Dr. Heung-Yeung Shum and Dr. Yong Rui of Microsoft Research for the face motion data. Zhen Wen would also like to thank his parents and his wife Xiaohui Gu, who have been supportive of his many years of education and the time and resources it has cost. Finally, we would like to thank Dr. Mubarak Shah and staff at Kluwer Academic Press for their help in preparing this book.

Chapter 1

INTRODUCTION

This book is concerned with the computational processing of 3D faces, with applications in Human Computer Interaction (HCI). It is a disciplinary research area overlapping with computer vision, computer graphics, machine learning and HCI. Various aspects of 3D face processing research are addressed in this book. For these aspects, we will both survey existing methods and present our research results.

In the first chapter, this book introduces the motivation and background of 3D face processing research and gives an overview of our research. Several research topics will be discussed in more details in the following chapters. First, we describe methods and systems for modeling the geometry of static 3D face surfaces. Such static models lay basis for both 3D face analysis and synthesis. To study the motion of human faces, we propose motion models derived from geometric motion data. Then, the models could be used for both analysis (e.g. tracking) and synthesis (e.g. animation). In these geometric motion models, appearance variations caused by motion are missing. However, these appearance changes are important for both human perception and computer analysis. Therefore, in the next part of the book, we propose a flexible appearance model to enhance the face processing framework. The flexible appearance model enables efficient and effective treatment of illumination effects and person-dependency. We will present experimental results to show the efficacy of our face processing framework in various applications, such as very low bit-rate face video coding, facial expression recognition, intelligent HCI environment and etc. Finally this book discusses future research directions of face processing.

In the remaining sections of this chapter, we discuss the motivation for 3D face processing research and then give overviews of our 3D face processing research.

1.   Motivation

Human face provides important visual cues for effective face-to-face human-human communication. In human-computer interaction (HCI) and distant human-human interaction, computer can use face processing techniques to estimate users' states information, based on face cues extracted from video sensor. Such states information is useful for the computer to proactively initiate appropriate actions. On the other hand, graphics based face animation provides an effective solution for delivering and displaying multimedia information related to human face. Therefore, the advance in the computational model of faces would make human computer interaction more effective. Examples of the applications that may benefit from face processing techniques include: visual telecommunication [Aizawa and Huang, 1995, Morishima, 1998], virtual environments [Leung et al., 2000], and talking head representation of agents [Waters et al., 1996, Pandzic et al., 1999].

Recently, security related issues have become major concerns in both research and application domains. Video surveillance has become increasingly critical to ensuring security. Intelligent video surveillance, which uses automatic visual analysis techniques, can relieve human operators from the labor-intensive monitoring tasks [Hampapur et al., 2003]. It would also enhance the system capabilities for prevention and investigation of suspicious behaviors. One important group of automatic visual analysis techniques are face processing techniques, such as face detection, tracking and recognition.

2.   Research Topics Overview

2.1   3D face processing framework overview

In the field of face processing, there are two research directions: analysis and synthesis. Research issues and their applications are illustrated in Figure 1.1. For analysis, firstly face needs to be located in input video. Then, the face image can be used to identify who the person is. The face motion in the video can also be tracked. The estimated motion parameters can be used for user monitoring or emotion recognition. Besides, the face motion can also be used to as visual features in audio-visual speech recognition, which has higher recognition rate than audio-only recognition in noisy environments. The face motion analysis and synthesis is an important issue of the framework. In this book, the motions include both rigid and non-rigid motions. Our main focus is the non-rigid motions such as the motions caused by speech or expressions, which are more complex and challenging. We use "facial deformation model" or "facial motion model" to refer to non-rigid motion model, if without other clarification.

The other research direction is synthesis. First, the geometry of neutral face is modeled from measurement of faces, such as 3D range scanner data or images. Then, the 3D face model is deformed according to facial deformation model

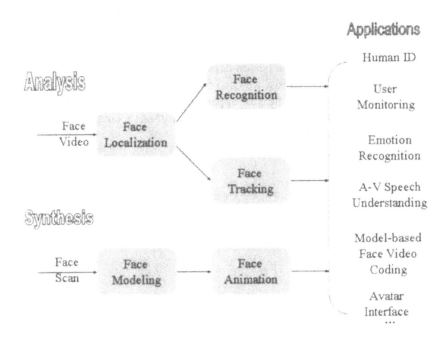

Figure 1.1. Research issues and applications of face processing.

to produce animation. The animation may be used as avatar-based interface for human computer interaction. One particular application is model-based face video coding. The idea is to analyze face video and only transmit a few motion parameters, and maybe some residual. Then the receiver can synthesize corresponding face appearance based on the motion parameters. This scheme can achieve better visual quality under very low bit-rate.

In this book, we present a 3D face processing framework for both analysis and synthesis. The framework is illustrated in Figure 1.2. Due to the complexity of facial motion, we first collect 3D facial motion data using motion capture devices. Then subspace learning method is applied to derive a few basis. We call these basis Geometric Motion Units, or simply MUs. Any facial shapes can be approximated by a linear combination of the Motion Units. In face motion analysis, the MU subspace can be used to constrain noisy 2D image motion for more robust estimation. In face animation, MUs can be used to reconstruct facial shapes. The MUs, however, are only able to model geometric facial motion because appearance details are usually missing in motion capture data. These appearance details caused by motion are important for both human perception and computer analysis. To handle the motion details, we incorporate appearance model in the framework. We have focused on the problem of how to make the appearance model more flexible so that it can be used in various conditions. For this purpose, we have developed efficient methods for modeling the illumination effects and reduce the person-dependency of the appearance model. To evaluate face motion analysis, we have done facial expression recognition experiments to show that the flexible appearance model improve the results under varying conditions. We shall also present synthesis examples using the flexible appearance model.

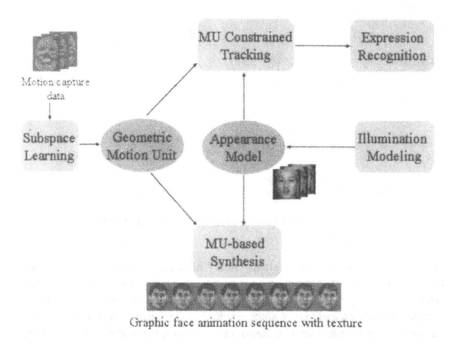

Graphic face animation sequence with texture

Figure 1.2.   A unified 3D face processing framework.

2.2   3D face geometry modeling

Generating 3D human face models has been a persistent challenge in both computer vision and computer graphics. A 3D face model lays basis for model-based face video analysis and facial animations. In face video analysis, a 3D face model helps recognition of oblique views of faces [Blanz et al., 2002]. Based on the 3D geometric model of faces, facial deformation models can be constructed for 3D non-rigid face tracking [DeCarlo, 1998, Tao, 1999]. In computer graphics, 3D face models can be deformed to produce animations.

The animations are essential to computer games, film making, online chat, virtual presence, video conferencing, etc.

There have been many methods proposed for modeling the 3D geometry of faces. Traditionally, people have used interactive design tools to build human face models. To reduce the labor-intensive manual work, people have applied prior knowledge such as anthropometry knowledge [DeCarlo et al., 1998]. More recently, because 3D sensing techniques become available, more realistic models can be derived based on those 3D measurement of faces. So far, the most popular commercially available tools are those using laser scanners. However, these scanners are usually expensive. Moreover, the data are usually noisy, requiring extensive hand touch-up and manual registration before the model can be used in analysis and synthesis. Because inexpensive computers and image/video sensors are widely available nowadays, there is great interest in producing face models directly from images. In spite of progress toward this goal, this type of techniques are still computationally expensive and need manual intervention.

In this book, we will give an overview of these 3D face modeling techniques. Then we will describe the tools in our iFACE system for building personalized 3D face models. The iFACE system is a 3D face modeling and animation system, developed based on the 3D face processing framework. It takes the $Cyberware^{TM}$ 3D scanner data of a subject's head as input and provides a set of tools to allow the user to interactively fit a generic face model to the $Cyberware^{TM}$ scanner data. Later in this book, we show that these models can be effectively used in model-based 3D face tracking, and 3D face synthesis such as text- and speech-driven face animation.

2.3 Geometric-based facial motion modeling, analysis and synthesis

Accurate face motion analysis and realistic face animation demands good model of the temporal and spatial facial deformation. One type of approaches use geometric-based models [Black and Yacoob, 1995, DeCarlo and Metaxas, 2000, Essa and Pentland, 1997, Tao and Huang, 1999, Terzopoulos and Waters, 1990a]. Geometric facial motion model describes the macrostructure level face geometry deformation. The deformation of 3D face surfaces can be represented using the displacement vectors of face surface points (i.e. vertices). In free-form interpolation models [Hong et al., 2001a, Tao and Huang, 1999], displacement vectors of certain points are predefined using interactive editing tools. The displacement vectors of the remaining face points are generated using interpolation functions, such as affine functions, radial basis functions (RBF), and Bezier volume. In physics-based models [Waters, 1987], the face vertices displacements are generated by dynamics equations. The parameters of these dynamic equations are manually tuned. To obtain a higher level of abstraction of facial motions which may facilitate semantic analysis, psychologists have proposed Facial Action Coding System (FACS) [Ekman and Friesen, 1977]. FACS is based on anatomical studies on facial muscular activity and it enumerates all Action Units (AUs) of a face that cause facial movements. Currently, FACS is widely used as the underlying visual representation for facial motion analysis, coding, and animation. The Action Units, however, lack quantitative definition and temporal description. Therefore, computer scientists usually need to decide their own definition in their computational models of AUs [Tao and Huang, 1999]. Because of the high complexity of natural non-rigid facial motion, these models usually need extensive manual adjustments to achieve realistic results.

Recently, there have been considerable advances in motion capture technology. It is now possible to collect large amount of real human motion data. For example, the $MotionAnalysis^{TM}$ system [MotionAnalysis, 2002] uses multiple high speed cameras to track 3D movement of reflective markers. The motion data can be used in movies, video game, industrial measurement, and research in movement analysis. Because of the increasingly available motion capture data, people begin to apply machine learning techniques to learn motion model from the data. This type of models would capture the characteristics of real human motion. One example is the linear subspace models of facial motion learned in [Kshirsagar et al., 2001, Hong et al., 2001b, Reveret and Essa, 2001]. In these models, arbitrary face deformation can be approximated by a linear combination of the learn basis.

In this book, we present our 3D facial deformation models derived from motion capture data. Principal component analysis (PCA) [Jolliffe, 1986] is applied to extract a few basis whose linear combinations explain the major variations in the motion capture data. We call these basis Motion Units (MUs), in a similar spirit to AUs. Compared to AUs, MUs are derived automatically from motion capture data such that it avoids the labor-intensive manual work for designing AUs. Moreover, MUs has smaller reconstruction error than AUs when linear combinations are used to approximate arbitrary facial shapes. Based on MUs, we have developed a 3D non-rigid face tracking system. The subspace spanned by MUs is used to constrain the noisy image motion estimation, such as optical flow. As a result, the estimated non-rigid can be more robust. We demonstrate the efficacy of the tracking system in model-based very low bit-rate face video coding. The linear combinations of MUs can also be used to deform 3D face surface for face animations. In iFACE system, we have developed text-driven face animation and speech-driven animations. Both of them use MUs as the underlying representation of face deformation. One particular type of animation is real-time speech-driven face animation, which is useful for real-time two-way communications such as teleconferencing. We have used MUs as the visual representation to learn a audio-to-visual mapping. The mapping has a delay of only 100 ms, which will not interfere with real-time two-way communications.

2.4 Enhanced facial motion analysis and synthesis using flexible appearance model

Besides the geometric deformations modeled from motion capture data, facial motions also exhibit detailed appearance changes such as wrinkles and creases as well. These details are important visual cues but they are difficult to analyze and synthesize using geometric-based approaches. Appearance-based models have been adopted to deal with this problem [Bartlett et al., 1999, Donato et al., 1999]. Previous appearance-based approaches were mostly based on extensive training appearance examples. However, the space of all face appearance is huge, affected by the variations across different head poses, individuals, lighting, expressions, speech and etc. Thus it is difficult for appearance-based methods to collect enough face appearance data and train a model that works robustly in many different scenarios. In this respect, the geometric-feature-based methods are more robust to large head motions, changes of lighting and are less person-dependent.

To combine the advantages of both approaches, people have been investigating methods of using both geometry (shape) and appearance (texture) in face analysis and synthesis. The Active Appearance Model (AAM) [Cootes et al., 1998] and its variants, apply PCA to model both the shape variations of image patches and their texture variations. They have been shown to be powerful tools for face alignment, recognition, and synthesis. Blanz and Vetter [Blanz and Vetter, 1999] propose 3D morphable models for 3D faces modeling, which model the variations of both 3D face shape and texture using PCA. The 3D morphable models have been shown effective in 3D face animation and face recognition from non-frontal views [Blanz et al., 2002]. In facial expression classification, Tian et al. [Tian et al., 2002] and Zhang et al. [Zhang et al., 1998] propose to train classifiers (e.g. neural networks) using both shape and texture features. The trained classifiers were shown to outperform classifiers using shape or texture features only. In these approaches, some variations of texture are absorbed by shape variation models. However, the potential texture space can still be huge because many other variations are not modelled by shape model. Moreover, little has been done to adapt the learned models to new conditions. As a result, the application of these methods are limited to conditions similar to those of training data.

In this book, we propose a flexible appearance model in our framework to deal with detailed facial motions. We have developed an efficient method for modeling illumination effects from a single face image. We also apply ratio-image technique [Liu et al., 2001a] to reduce person-dependency in a principled way. Using these two techniques, we design novel appearance features and use them in facial motion analysis. In a facial expression experiment using CMU Cohn-Kanade database [Kanade et al., 2000], we show that the the novel appearance features can deal with motion details in a less illumination dependent and person-dependent way [Wen and Huang, 2003]. In face synthesis, the flexible appearance model enables us to transfer motion details and lighting effects from one person to another [Wen et al., 2003]. Therefore, the appearance model constructed in one conditions can be extended to other conditions. Synthesis examples show the effectiveness of the approach.

2.5   Applications of face processing framework

3D face processing techniques have many applications ranging from intelligent human computer interaction to smart video surveillance. In this book, besides face processing techniques we will discuss applications of our 3D face processing framework to demonstrate the effectiveness of the framework.

The first application is model-based very low bit-rate face video coding. Nowadays Internet has become an important part of people's daily life. In the current highly heterogeneous network environments, a wide range of bandwidth is possible. Provisioning for good video quality at very low bit rates is an important yet challenging problem. One alternative approach to the traditional waveform-based video coding techniques is the model-based coding approach. In the emerging Motion Picture Experts Group 4 (MPEG-4) standard, a model-based coding standard has been established for face video. The idea is to create a 3D face model and encode the variations of the video as parameters of the 3D model. Initially the sender sends the model to the receiver. After that, the sender extracts the motion parameters of the face model in the incoming face video. These motion parameters can be transmitted to the receiver under very low bit-rate. Then the receiver can synthesize corresponding face animation using the motion parameters. However, in most existing approaches following the MPEG-4 face animation standard, the residual is not sent so that the synthesized face image could be very different from the original image. In this book, we propose a hybrid approach to solve this problem. On one hand, we use our 3D face tracking to extract motion parameters for model-based video coding. On the other hand, we use the waveform-based video coder to encode the residual and background. In this way, the difference between the reconstructed frame and the original frame is bounded and can be controlled. The experimental results show that our hybrid deliver better performance under very low bit-rate than the state-of-the-art waveform-based video codec.

The second application is to use face processing techniques in an integrated human computer interaction environment. In this project the goal is to contribute to the development of a human-computer interaction environment in which the computer detects and tracks the user's emotional, motivational, cognitive and task states, and initiates communications based on this knowledge, rather than simply responding to user commands. In this environment, the test-bed is to teach school kids scientific principles via LEGO games. In this learning task, the kids are taught to put gears together so that they can learn principles about ratio and forces. In this HCI environment, we use face tracking and facial expression techniques to estimate the users' states. Moreover, we use animated 3D synthetic face as avatar to interact with the kids. In this book, we describe the experiment we have done so far and the lessons we have learned in this process.

3. Book Organization

The remainder of the book is organized as follows. In the next chapter, we first give a review on the work in 3D face modeling. Then we present our tools for modeling personalized 3D face geometry. Such 3D models will be used throughout our framework. Chapter 3 introduces our 3D facial motion database and the derivation of the geometric motion model. In Chapter 4, we describe how to use the derived geometric facial motion model to achieve robust 3D non-rigid face tracking. We will present experimental results in a model-based very low bit-rate face video coding application. We shall present the facial motion synthesis using the learned geometric motion model in Chapter 5. Three types of animation are described: (1) text-driven face animation; (2) offline speech-driven animation; and (3) real-time speech driven animation. Chapter 6 presents our flexible appearance model for dealing with motion details in our face processing framework. An efficient method is proposed to model illumination effects from a single face image. The illumination model helps reduce the illumination dependency of the appearance model. We also present ratio-image based techniques to reduce person-dependency of our appearance model. In Chapter 7 and Chapter 8, we describe our works on coping with appearance details in analysis and synthesis based on the flexible appearance model. Experimental results on facial expression recognition and face synthesis in varying conditions are presented to demonstrate the effectiveness of the flexible appearance model. Finally, the book is concluded with summary and comments on future research directions.

Chapter 2

3D FACE MODELING

In this chapter, we first review works on modeling 3D geometry of static human faces in Section 1. Then, we introduce the face modeling tools in our iFACE system. The models will later be used as the foundation for face analysis and face animation in our 3D face processing framework. Finally, in Section 3, we discuss future directions of 3D face modeling.

1.   State of the Art

Facial modeling has been an active research topic of computer graphics and computer vision for over three decades [DiPaola, 1991, Fua and Miccio, 1998, Lee et al., 1993, Lee et al., 1995, Lewis, 1989, Magneneat-Thalmann et al., 1989, Parke, 1972, Parke, 1974, Parke and Waters, 1996, Badler and Platt, 1981, Terzopoulos and Waters, 1990b, Todd et al., 1980, Waters, 1987]. A complete overview can be found in Parke and Waters' book [Parke and Waters, 1996]. Traditionally, people have used interactive design tools to build human face models. To reduce the labor-intensive manual work, people have applied prior knowledge about human face geometry. DeCarlo et al. [DeCarlo et al., 1998] proposed a method to generate face models based on face measurements randomly generated according to anthropometric statistics. They showed that they were able to generate a variety of face geometries using these face measurements as constraints. With the advance of sensor technologies, people have been able to measure the 3D geometry of human faces using 3D range scanners, or reconstruct 3D faces from multiple 2D images using computer vision techniques. In Section 1.1 and 1.2, we give a review of the works of these two approaches.

1.1   Face modeling using 3D range scanner

Recently, laser-based 3D range scanners have been commercially available. Examples include $Cyberware^{TM}$ [Cyberware, 2003] scanner, $Eyetronics^{TM}$ scanner [Eyetronics, 2003], and etc. $Cyberware^{TM}$ scanner shines a safe, low-intensity laser on a human face to create a lighted profile. A video sensor captures this profile from two viewpoints. The laser beam rotates around the face 360 degrees in less than 30 seconds so that the 3D shape of the face can captured by combining the profiles from every angle. Simultaneously, a second video sensor in the scanner acquires color information. $Eyetronics^{TM}$ scanner shines a laser grid onto the human facial surface. Based on the deformation of the grid, the geometry of the surface is computed. Comparing these two systems, $Eyetronics^{TM}$ is a "one shot" system which can output 3D face geometry based on the data of a single shot. In contrast, $Cyberware^{TM}$ scanner need to collect multiple profiles in a full circle which takes more time. In post-processing stage, however, $Eyetronics^{TM}$ needs more manual adjustment to deal with noisy data. As for the captured texture of the 3D model, $Eyetronics^{TM}$ has higher resolution since it uses high resolution digital camera, while texture in $Cyberware^{TM}$ has lower resolution because it is derived from low resolution video sensor. In summary, these two ranger scanners have different features and can be used to capture 3D face data in different scenarios.

Based on the 3D measurement using these ranger scanners, many approaches have been proposed to generate 3D face models ready for animation. Ostermann et al. [Ostermann et al., 1998] developed a system to fit a 3D model using $Cyberware^{TM}$ scan data. Then the model is used for MPEG-4 face animation. Lee et al. [Lee et al., 1993, Lee et al., 1995] developed techniques to clean up and register data generated from $Cyberware^{TM}$ laser scanners. The obtained model is then animated by using a physically based approach. Marschner et al. [Marschner et al., 2000] achieved the model fitting using a method built upon fitting subdivision surfaces.

1.2   Face modeling using 2D images

A number of researchers have proposed to create face models from 2D images. Some approaches use two orthogonal views so that the 3D information of facial surface points can be measured [Akimoto et al., 1993, Dariush et al., 1998, H.S.Ip and Yin, 1996]. They require two cameras which must be carefully set up so that their directions are orthogonal. Zheng [Zheng, 1994] developed a system to construct geometrical object models from image contours. The system requires a turn-table setup. Pighin et al. [Pighin et al., 1998] developed a system to allow a user to manually specify correspondences across multiple images, and use computer vision techniques to compute 3D reconstructions of specified feature points. A 3D mesh model is then fitted to the reconstructed 3D points. With a manually intensive procedure, they were able to generate highly realistic face models. Fua and Miccio [Fua and Miccio, 1998] developed system which combine multiple image measurements, such as stereo data, silhouette edges and 2D feature points, to reconstruct 3D face models from images.

Because the 3D reconstructions of face points from images are either noisy or require extensive manual work, researcher have tried to use prior knowledge as constraints to help the image-based 3D face modeling. One important type of constraints is the "linear classes" constraint. Under this constrain, it assumes that arbitrary 3D face geometry can be represented by a linear combination of certain basic face geometries. The advantage of using linear class of objects is that it eliminates most of the non-natural faces and significantly reduces the search space. Vetter and Poggio [Vetter and Poggio, 1997] represented an arbitrary face image as a linear combination of some number of prototypes and used this representation (called linear object class) for image recognition, coding, and image synthesis. In their representative work, Blanz and Vetter [Blanz and Vetter, 1999] obtain the basis of the linear classes by applying Principal Component Analysis (PCA) to a 3D face model database. The database contains models of 200 Caucasian adults, half of which are male. The 3D models are generated by cleaning up, registering the $Cyberware^{TM}$ scan data. Given a new face image, a fitting algorithm is used to estimate the coefficients of the linear combination. They have demonstrated that linear classes of face geometries and images are very powerful in generating convincing 3D human face models from images. For this approach to achieve convincing results, it requires that the novel is similar to faces in the database and the feature points of the initial 3D model is roughly aligned with the input face image.

Because it is difficult to obtain a comprehensive and high quality 3D face database, other approaches have been proposed using the idea of "linear classes of face geometries". Kang and Jones [Kang and Jones, 1999] also use linear spaces of geometrical models to construct 3D face models from multiple images. But their approach requires manually aligning the generic mesh to one of the images, which is in general a tedious task for an average user. Instead of representing a face as a linear combination of real faces, Liu et al. [Liu et al., 2001b] represent it as a linear combination of a neutral face and some number of face metrics where a metric is a vector that linearly deforms a face. The metrics in their systems are meaningful face deformations, such as to make the head wider, make the nose bigger, etc. They are defined interactively by artists.

1.3 Summary

Among the many approaches for 3D face modeling, 3D range scanners provide high quality 3D measurements for building realistic face models. However, most scanners are still very expensive and need to be used in controlled environments. In contrast, image-based approaches have low cost and can be used in more general conditions. But the 3D measurements in image-based approaches are much noisier which could degrade the quality of the reconstructed 3D model. Therefore, for applications which need 3D face models, it is desirable to have a comprehensive tool kit to process a variety of input data. The input data could be 3D scanner data, 2D images from one or multiple viewpoints. For our framework, we have developed tools for 3D face modeling from 3D range scanners. Using these tools, we have built 3D face model for face animation as avatar interface in human computer interaction, and psychological studies on human perceptions.

In Section 2, we will describe our face modeling tool for our face processing framework. After that, some future directions will be discussed in Section 3.

2.   Face Modeling Tools in iFACE

We have developed iFACE system which provides functionalities for face modeling and face animation. It provides a research platform for the 3D face processing framework. The iFACE system takes the $Cyberware^{TM}$ scanner data of a subject's head as input and allows the user to interactively fit a generic face model to the $Cyberware^{TM}$ scanner data. The iFACE system also provides tools for text-driven face animation and speech-driven face animation. The animation techniques will be described in Chapter 5.

2.1   Generic face model

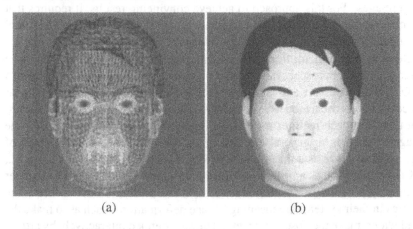

(a)   (b)

Figure 2.1. The generic face model. (a): Shown as wire-frame model. (b): Shown as shaded model.

The generic face model in the iFACE system consists of nearly all the head components such as face, eyes, teeth, ears, tongue, and etc. The surfaces of the components are approximated by triangular meshes. There are 2240 vertices and 2946 triangles. The tongue component is modeled by a Non-Uniform

Rational B-Splines (NURBS) model which has 63 control points. The generic face model is illustrated in Figure 2.1.

2.2 Personalized face model

In iFACE, the process of making a personalized face model is nearly automatic with only a few manual adjustments necessary. To customize the face model for a particular person, we first obtain both the texture data and range data of that person by scanning his/her head using $Cyberware^{TM}$ range scanner. An example of the range scanner data is shown in Figure 2.2.

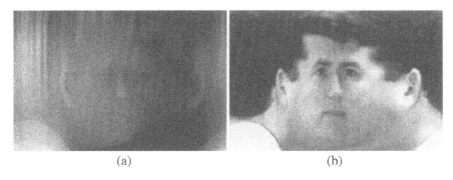

(a)   (b)

Figure 2.2. An example of range scanner data. (a): Range map. (b): Texture map.

Figure 2.3. Feature points defined on texture map.

We define thirty-five facial feature points on the face surface of the generic head model. If we unfold the face component of the head model onto 2D, those feature points triangulate the face mesh into several local patches. The 2D locations of the feature points in the range map are manually selected on the scanned texture data, which are shown in Figure 2.3. The system calculates the 2D positions of the remaining face mesh vertices on the range map by deforming the local patches based on the range data. By collecting the range information according to the positions of the vertices on the range map, the 3D facial geometry is decided. The remaining head components are automatically adjust by shifting, rotating, and scaling. Interactive manual editing on the fitted model are required where the scanned data are missing. We have developed an interactive model editing tools to make the editing easy. The interface of the editing tool is shown in Figure 2.4. After editing, texture map is mapped onto

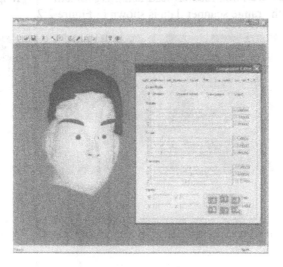

Figure 2.4.   The model editor.

the customized model to achieve photo-realistic appearance. Figure 2.5 shows an example of a customized face model.

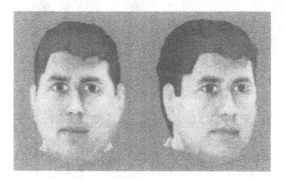

Figure 2.5.   An example of customized face models.

3. Future Research Direction of 3D Face Modeling

In the future, one promising research direction is to improve face modeling tools which use one face image, along the line of the "linear class geometries" work [Blanz and Vetter, 1999]. Improvements in the following aspects are highly desirable.

- 3D face databases: The expressiveness of the "linear class geometries" approach is decided by the 3D face model databases. In order to generate convincing 3D face models for more people other than young Caucasian in the Blanz and Vetter'99 database [Blanz and Vetter, 1999], more 3D face scan data are needed to be collected for people of different races and different ages.

- Registration techniques for images and models: For the collected 3D face geometries and textures, the corresponding facial points need to be aligned. This registration process is required before linear subspace model can be learned. This registration is also required for reconstructing a 3D face model from an input face image. The original registration technique in [Blanz and Vetter, 1999] is computationally expensive and need good initialization. More recently, Romdhani and Vetter improved the efficiency, robustness and accuracy of the registration process in [Romdhani and Vetter, 2003]. Recent automatic facial feature localization techniques can also help the automatic generation of 3D face models [Hu et al., 2004].

- Subspace modeling: When the 3D face database includes more geometry variations, PCA may no longer be a good way to model the face geometry subspace. Other subspace learning methods, such as Independent Component Analysis (ICA) [Comon, 1994], local PCA [Kambhatla and Leen, 1997], need to explored the find better subspace representation.

- Illumination effects of texture model: The textures of the 3D face models also need to be collected to model the appearance variation, as in [Blanz and Vetter, 1999]. Because illumination affects face appearance significantly, the illumination effects need to be modeled. Besides the illumination models in Blanz and Vetter's work [Blanz and Vetter, 1999], recent advances in theoretical studies of illumination have enabled more efficient and effective methods. In this book, we present an efficient illumination modeling method based on a single input face image. This method is discussed in details in Chapter 6.

Chapter 3

LEARNING GEOMETRIC 3D FACIAL MOTION MODEL

In this section, we introduce the method for learning geometric 3D facial motion model in our framework. 3D facial motion model describes the spatial and temporal deformation of 3D facial surface. Efficient and effective facial motion analysis and synthesis requires a compact yet powerful model to capture real facial motion characteristics. For this purpose, analysis of real facial motion data is needed because of the high complexity of human facial motion.

We first give a review of previous works on 3D face motion models in Section 1. Then, in Section 2, we introduce the motion capture database used in our framework. Section 3 and 4 present our methods for learning *holistic* and *parts-based* spatial geometric facial motion models, respectively. Section 5 introduces how we apply the learned models to arbitrary face mesh. Finally, in Section 6, we brief describe the temporal facial motion modeling in our framework.

1. Previous Work

Since the pioneering work of Parke [Parke, 1972] in the early 70's, many techniques have been investigated to model facial deformation for 3D face tracking and animation. A good survey can be found in [Parke and Waters, 1996]. The key issues include (1) how to model the spatial and temporal facial surface deformation, and (2) how to apply these models for facial deformation analysis and synthesis. In this section, we introduce previous research on facial deformation modeling.

1.1 Facial deformation modeling

In the past several decades, many models have been proposed to deform 3D facial surface spatially. Representative models include free-form interpolation models [Hong et al., 2001a, Tao and Huang, 1999], parameterized models [Parke, 1974], physics-based models [Waters, 1987], and more recently machine-learning-based models [Kshirsagar et aι., 2001, Hong et al., 2001b, Reveret and Essa, 2001]. Free-form interpolation models define a set of points as control points, and then use the displacement of the control points to interpolate the movements of any facial surface points. Popular interpolation functions includes: affine functions [Hong et al., 2001a], Splines, radial basis functions, Bezier volume model [Tao and Huang, 1999] and others. Parameterized models (such as Parke's model [Parke, 1974] and its descendants) use facial feature based parameters for customized interpolation functions. Physics-based muscle models [Waters, 1987] use dynamics equations to model facial muscles. The face deformation can then be determined by solving those equations. Because of the high complexity of natural facial motion, these models usually need extensive manual adjustments to achieve plausible facial deformation. To approximate the space of facial deformation, people proposed linear subspaces based on Facial Action Coding System (FACS) [Essa and Pentland, 1997, Tao and Huang, 1999]. FACS [Ekman and Friesen, 1977] describes arbitrary facial deformation as a combination of Action Units (AUs) of a face. Because AUs are only defined qualitatively, and do not contain temporal information, they are usually manually customized for computation. Brand [Brand, 2001] used low-level image motion to learn a linear subspace model from raw video. However, the estimated low-level image motion is noisy such that the derived model is less realistic. With the recent advance in motion capture technology, it is now possible to collect large amount of real human motion data. Thus, people turn to apply machine learning techniques to learn model from motion capture data, which would capture the characteristics of real human motion. Some examples of this type of approaches are discussed in Section 1.3.

1.2   Facial temporal deformation modeling

For face animation and tracking, temporal facial deformation also needs to be modeled. Temporal facial deformation model describes the temporal trajectory of facial deformation, given constraints at certain time instances. Waters and Levergood [Waters and Levergood, 1993] used sinusoidal interpolation scheme for temporal modeling. Pelachaud et al. [Pelachaud et al., 1991], Cohen and Massaro [Cohen and Massaro, 1993] customized co-articulation functions based on prior knowledge, to model the temporal trajectory between given key shapes. Physics-based methods solve dynamics equations for these trajectories.

Recently, statistical methods have been applied in facial temporal deformation modeling. Hidden Markov Models (HMM) trained from motion capture data are shown to be useful to capture the dynamics of natural facial deformation [Brand, 1999]. Ezzat et al. [Ezzat et al., 2002] pose the trajectory modeling problem as a regularization problem [Wahba, 1990]. The goal is to synthesize a trajectory which minimizes an objective function consisting of a target term and a smoothness term. The target term is a distance function between the trajectory and the given key shapes. The optimization of the objective function yields *multivariate additive quintic splines* [Wahba, 1990]. The results produced by this approach could look under-articulated. To solve this problem, gradient descent learning [Bishop, 1995] is employed to adjust the mean and covariances. In the learning process, the goal is to reduce the difference between the synthesized trajectories and the trajectories in the training data. Experimental results show that the learning improves the articulation.

1.3 Machine learning techniques for facial deformation modeling

In recent years, more available facial motion capture data enables researchers to learn models which capture the characteristics of real facial deformation.

Artificial Neural Network (ANN) is a powerful tool to approximate functions. It has been used to approximate the functional relationship between motion capture data and the parameters of pre-defined facial deformation models. Morishima et al. [Morishima et al., 1998] used ANN to learn a function, which maps 2D marker movements to the parameters of a physics-based 3D face deformation model. This helped to automate the construction of physics-based face muscle model, and to improve the animation produced. Moreover, ANN has been used to learn the correlation between facial deformation and other related signals. For example, ANN is used to map speech to face animation [Lavagetto, 1995, Morishima and Yotsukura, 1999, Massaro and et al., 1999].

Principal Component Analysis (PCA) [Jolliffe, 1986] learns orthogonal components that explain the maximum amount of variance in a given data set. Because facial deformation is complex yet structured, PCA has been applied to learn a compact low dimensional linear subspace representation of 3D face deformation [Hong et al., 2001b, Kshirsagar et al., 2001, Reveret and Essa, 2001]. Then, arbitrary complex face deformation can be approximated by a linear combination of just a few basis vectors. Besides animation, the low dimensional linear subspace can be used to constrain noisy low-level motion estimation to achieve more robust 3D facial motion analysis [Hong et al., 2001b, Reveret and Essa, 2001]. Furthermore, facial deformation is known to be localized. To learn a localized subspace representation of facial deformation, Non-negative Matrix Factorization (NMF) [Lee and Seung, 1999] could be used. It has been shown that NMF and its variants are effective to learn parts-based face image components, which outperform PCA in face recognition when there are occlusions [Li and et al., 2001]. In this chapter, we describe how NMF may help to learn a parts-based facial deformation model. The advantage of a parts-based model is its flexibility in local facial motion analysis and synthesis.

The dynamics of facial motion is complex so that it is difficult to model with dynamics equations. Data-driven model, such as Hidden Markov Model (HMM) [Rabiner, 1989], provides an effective alternative. One example is "voice puppetry" [Brand, 1999], where an HMM trained by entropy minimization is used to model the dynamics of facial motion during speech. Then, the HMM model is used to off-line generate a smooth facial deformation trajectory given speech signal.

2. Motion Capture Database

To study the complex motion of face during speech and expression, we need an extensive motion capture database. The database can be used to learn facial motion models. Furthermore, it will benefit future study on bimodal speech perception, synthetic talking head development and evaluation and etc. In our framework, we have experimented on both data collected using $MotionAnalysis^{TM}$ system, and the facial motion capture data provided by Dr. Brian Guenter [Guenter et al., 1998] of Microsoft Research.

MotionAnalysis [MotionAnalysis, 2002] **EvaRT 3.2** system is a marker-based capture device, which can be used for capturing geometric facial deformation. An example of the marker layout is shown in Figure 3.1. There are 44 markers on the face. Such marker-based capture devices have high temporal

Figure 3.1.   An example of marker layout for MotionAnalysis system.

resolution (up to 300fps), however the spatial resolution is low (only tens of markers on face are feasible). Appearance details due to facial deformation, therefore, is handled using our flexible appearance model presented in chapter 6.

The Microsoft data, collected by by Guenter et al. [Guenter et al., 1998], use 153 markers. Figure 3.2 shows an example of the markers. For better visualization purpose, we build a mesh based on those markers, illustrated by Figure 3.2 (b) and (c).

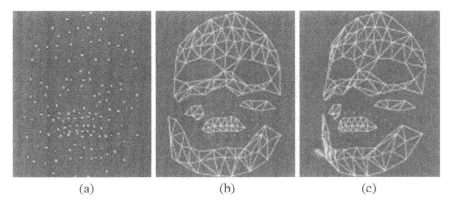

Figure 3.2. The markers of the Microsoft data [Guenter et al., 1998]. (a): The markers are shown as small white dots. (b) and (c): The mesh is shown in two different viewpoints.

3. Learning Holistic Linear Subspace

To make complex facial deformation tractable in computational models, people have usually assumed that any facial deformation can be approximated by a linear combination of some basic deformation. In our framework, we make the same assumption, and try to find optimal bases under this assumption. We call these bases *Motion Units* (MUs). Using MUs, a facial shape $\vec{s}$ can be represented by

$$\vec{s} = \vec{s}_0 + (\sum_{i=1}^{M} c_i \vec{e}_i + \vec{e}_0) \tag{3.1}$$

where $\vec{s}_0$ denotes the facial shape without deformation, $\vec{e}_0$ is the mean facial deformation, $\{\vec{e}_0, \vec{e}_1, ..., \vec{e}_M\}$ is the MU set, and $\{c_1, c_2, ..., c_M\}$ is the MU parameter (MUP) set.

In this book, we experiment on both of the two databases described in Section 2. Principal Component Analysis (PCA) [Jolliffe, 1986] is applied to learning MUs from the database. The mean facial deformation and the first seven eigenvectors of PCA results are selected as the MUs. The MUs correspond to the largest seven eigenvalues that capture 93.2% of the facial deformation variance, The first four MUs are visualized by an animated face model in Figure 3.3. The top row images are the frontal views of the faces, and the bottom row images are side views. The first face is the neutral face, corresponding to $\vec{s}_0$. The remaining faces are deformed by the first four MUs scaled by a constant (from left to right). The method for visualizing MUs is described in Section 5. Any arbitrary facial deformation can be approximated by a linear combination of the MUs, weighted by MUPs. MUs are used in robust 3D facial motion analysis presented in Chapter 4, and facial motion synthesis presented in Chapter 5.

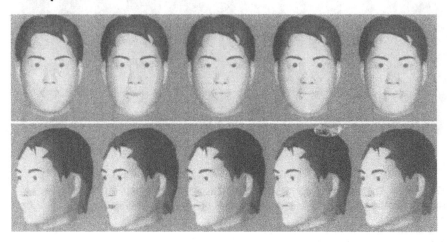

Figure 3.3.   The neutral face and deformed face corresponding to the first four MUs. The top row is frontal view and the bottom row is side view.

4.   Learning Parts-based Linear Subspace

It is well known that the facial motion is localized, which makes it possible to decompose the complex facial motion into smaller parts. The decomposition helps: (1) reduce the complexity in deformation modeling; (2) improve the robustness in motion analysis; and (3) flexibility in synthesis. The decomposition can be done manually based on the prior knowledge of facial muscle distribution, such as in [Pighin et al., 1999, Tao and Huang, 1999]. However, the decomposition may not be optimal for the linear combination model used because of the high nonlinearity of facial motion. Parts-based learning techniques, together with extensive motion capture data, provide a way to help design *parts-based facial deformation models*, which can better approximate real local facial motion. Recently several learning techniques have been proposed for learning representation of data samples that appears to be localized. Non-negative matrix Factorization (NMF) [Lee and Seung, 1999] has been shown to be able to learn basis images that resemble parts of faces. In learning the basis of subspace, NMF imposes non-negativity constraints, which is compatible to the intuitive notion of combining parts to form a whole in a non-subtractive way.

In our framework, we present a parts-based face deformation model. In the model, each part corresponds to a facial region where facial motion is mostly generated by local muscles. The motion of each part is modeled by PCA as described in Section 3. Then, the overall facial deformation is approximated by summing up the deformation in each part:

$$\Delta \vec{s} = \sum_{j=1}^{N} \Delta \vec{s}_j = \sum_{j=1}^{N} (\sum_{i=1}^{M_j} c_{ij} \vec{e}_{ij} + \vec{e}_{0j}) \tag{3.2}$$

where $\Delta \vec{s} = \vec{s} - \vec{s}_0$ is the deformation of the facial shape. N is the number of parts. We call this representation *parts-based MU*, where the j-th part has its MU set $\{\vec{e}_{0j}, \vec{e}_{1j}, ..., \vec{e}_{Mj}\}$, and MUP set $\{c_{1j}, c_{2j}, ..., c_{Mj}\}$.

To decompose facial motion into parts, we use NMF together with prior knowledge. In this method, we randomly initialize the decomposition. Then, we use NMF to reduce the linear decomposition error to a local minimum. We impose the non-negativity constraint in the linear combination of the facial motion energy. We use a matlab implementation of NMF from the web site *http://journalclub.mit.edu* (under category "Computational Neuroscience"). The algorithm is an iterative optimization process. In our experiments, we use 500 iterations. Figure 3.4(a) shows some parts derived by NMF. Adjacent different parts are shown in different patterns overlayed on the face model. We then use prior knowledge about facial muscle distribution to refine the learned parts. The parts can thus be (1) more related to meaningful facial muscle distribution, (2) less biased by individuality in the motion capture data, and (3) more easily generalized to different faces. We start with an image of human facial muscle distribution, illustrated in Figure 3.4(b) [FacialMuscel, 2002]. Next, we align it with our generic face model via image warping, based on facial feature points illustrated in Figure 3.7(c). The aligned facial muscle image is shown in Figure 3.4(c). Then, we overlay the learned parts on facial muscle distribution (Figure 3.4(d)), and adjust interactively the learned parts such that different parts correspond different muscles. The final parts are shown in Figure 3.4(e). The parts are overlapped a bit as learned by NMF. For convenience, the overlap is not shown Figure 3.4(e).

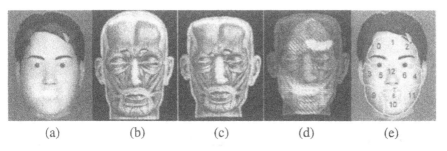

(a)   (b)   (c)   (d)   (e)

Figure 3.4. (a): NMF learned parts overlayed on the generic face model. (b): The facial muscle distribution. (c): The aligned facial muscle distribution. (d): The parts overlayed on muscle distribution. (e): The final parts decomposition.

The learned parts-based MUs give more flexibility in local facial deformation analysis and synthesis. Figure 3.5 and 3.6 show some local deformation in lower lips and right cheek, each of which is induced by one of the learned parts-based MUs. These locally deformed shapes are difficult to approximate using holistic MUs in Section 3. For each deformation shown in Figure 3.5 and 3.6, more

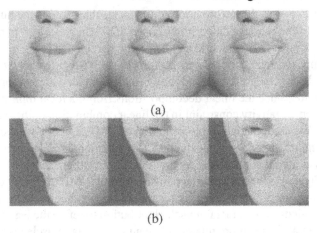

Figure 3.5. Three lower lips shapes deformed by three of the lower lips parts-based MUs respectively. The top row is the frontal view and the bottom row is the side view.

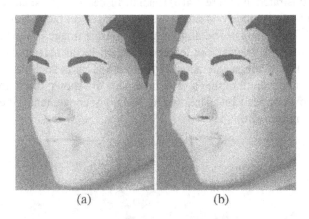

Figure 3.6. (a): The neutral face side view. (b): The face deformed by one right cheek parts-based MU.

than 100 holistic MUs are need to achieve a 90% reconst ·~⁺ion accuracy. That means, although some local deformation is induced by only one parts-based MU, more than 100 holistic MUs may be needed in order to achieve good analysis and synthesis quality. Therefore, we can have more flexibility in using parts-based MUs. For example, if we are only interested in motion in forehead, we only need to capture data about face with mainly forehead motion, and learn parts-based MUs from the data. In face animation, people often want to animate local region separately. This task can be easily achieved by adjusting MUPs of parts-based MUs separately. In face tracking, such as the system described in Chapter 4, people may use parts-based MUs to track only region of their interests (e.g. the lips). Furthermore, tracking using parts-based MUs is more robust because local error will not affect distant regions.

5.   Animate Arbitrary Mesh Using MU

The learned MUs are based the motion capture data of particular subjects. To use the MUs for other people, they need to be fitted to the new face geometry. Moreover, the MUs only sample the facial surface motion at the position of the markers. The movements at other places need to be interpolated. We call this process "MU" fitting.

In our framework, we use the face models generated by "iFACE" for MU-based face animation. "iFACE" is a face modeling and animation system developed in [Hong et al., 2001a]. The generic face model in iFACE is shown in Figure 3.7(a). Figure 3.7(b) shows a personalized model, which we customize based on the $Cyberware^{TM}$ scanner data for that person. Figure 3.7(c) shows the feature points we define on the iFACE generic model, which we use for MU fitting.

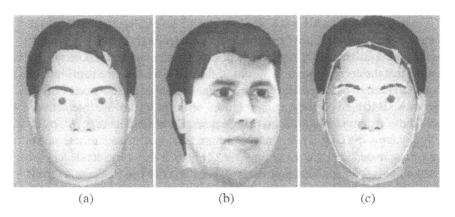

(a)   (b)   (c)

Figure 3.7.   (a): The generic model in iFACE. (b): A personalized face model based on the $Cyberware^{TM}$ scanner data. (c): The feature points defined on generic model.

In our previous work [Hong et al., 2002], we used MUs to animate models generated by iFACE. We dealt with the MU fitting problem by constructing a mapping between MUs and the face deformation model of iFACE. This technique allowed a key-frame based face animation system to use MUs. First we selected a set of training facial shapes with known MUPs. In a key-frame based animation system, these training shapes can be represented by linear combinations of key frames. Based on the equality between the two representations of the training shapes, the conversion between parameters of key-frame combination and MUPs could be derived as described in [Hong et al., 2002]. This method enabled us to use MUs for animation in a traditional key-frame-based animation system, such as iFACE. However, key frames of a certain system may not be expressive enough to take advantage of the motion details in MUs. Thus, the facial deformation information can be lost during conversion between parameters of key-frame combination and MUPs. Alternatively, interpolation-based techniques for re-targeting animation to new models, such as [Noh and Neumann, 2001], could be used for MU fitting. In similar spirit to [Noh and Neumann, 2001], we design our MU fitting as a two-step process: (1) face geometry based MU-adjustment; and (2) MU re-sampling. These two steps can be improved in a systematic way if enough MU sets are collected. For example, if MU statistics over a large set of different face geometries are available, one can systematically derive the geometry-to-MU mapping using machine-learning techniques. On the other hand, If multiple MU sets are available, which sample different positions of the same face, it is possible to combine them to increase the spatial resolution of MU because markers in MU are usually sparser than face geometry mesh.

The first step adjusts MUs to a face model with different geometry. The fundamental problem is to find a mapping from face geometry to MUs. Currently no data are available yet for MU statistics over different face geometry. We assume that the corresponding positions of the two faces have the same motion characteristics. Then, the adjustment is done by moving the markers of the learned MUs to their corresponding positions on the new face. We interactively build the correspondence of facial feature points shown in Figure 3.7(c) by labelling them via a GUI. Then, image warping technique is used to interpolate the correspondence in the remaining part. Note that the correspondences are based on only 2D facial feature locations, because only one image of a face is used in the GUI. We are working on using automatic facial feature localization techniques (e.g. [Hu et al., 2004]) to automate this step.

The second step is to derive movements of facial surface points that are not sampled by markers in MUs. This is essentially a signal re-sampling problem, for which an interpolation-based method is usually used. We use the popular radial basis interpolation function. The family of *radial basis functions* (RBF) is well known for its powerful interpolation capability. RBF is widely used in face model fitting [Pighin et al., 1998] and face animation [Guenter et al., 1998, Marschner et al., 2000, Noh and Neumann, 2001]. Using RBF, the displacement of a certain vertex $\vec{v}_i$ is of the form

$$\Delta \vec{v}_i = \sum_{j=1}^{N} w_{ij}\, h(\|\vec{v}_i - \vec{p}_j\|) \Delta \vec{p}_j \qquad (3.3)$$

where $\vec{p}_j, (j = 1, ..., N)$ is the coordinate of a marker, and $\Delta \vec{p}_j$ is its displacement. h is a radial basis kernel function such as Gaussian function, and w_{ij} are the weights. h and w_{ij} need to be carefully designed to ensure the interpolation quality. For facial deformation, the muscle influence region is local. Thus, we choose a cut-off region for each vertex. We set the weights to be zero for markers that are outside of the cut-off region, i.e., they are too far away to influence the vertex. In our current system, the local influence region for the i-th vertex is heuristically assigned as a circle, with the radius r_i as the average of the distances to its two nearest neighbors. Similar to [Marschner et al., 2000], we choose the radial basis kernel to be $h(x) = (1 + cos(\pi \frac{x}{r_i}))/2$, where $x = \|\vec{v}_i - \vec{p}_j\|$. We choose w_{ij} to be the normalization factor such that $\sum_{j=1}^{N} w_{ij} h(\|\vec{v}_i - \vec{p}_j\|) = 1$. The lips and eye lids are two special cases for this RBF interpolation, because the motions of upper parts of them are not correlated with the motions of the lower parts. To address this problem, we add "upper" or "lower" tags to vertices and markers near mouth and eyes. If a marker M and a vertex V have different tags, M has no influence on V. Thus, the weight of the marker M is set to be zero in the RBF interpolation (equation 3.3) of the vertex V. These RBF weights need to be computed only once for one set of marker positions. The weights are stored in a matrix. The matrix is sparse because marker influence is local. During synthesis, the movement of mesh vertices can be computed by one multiplication of the sparse RBF matrix based on equation 3.3. Thus the interpolation is fast.

After the MU fitting, MUs can be used to animate any 3D face models or analyze facial motion in image sequences. Deformed face image examples presented in this chapter, such as faces deformed by first four MUs in Figure 3.3, are produced after fitting MU to iFACE models. MU fitting is also used in facial motion analysis in Chapter 4.

6. Temporal Facial Motion Model

In this section, we describe the temporal facial deformation trajectory modeling in the 3D face processing framework. The model describes temporal variation of facial deformation given constraints (e.g. key shapes) at certain time instances. For compactness and usability, we propose to use an spline-based model similar to the spirit of the approach of Ezzat et al. [Ezzat et al., 2002]. The advantage of this approach is that it employs only a few key facial shapes estimated from training data. In order to get a smooth trajectory, we use NURBS (Nonuniform Rational B-splines) interpolation, which is easy to learn and perform well in general conditions. We also utilize the statistics of the training data in a way that covariance of the key shapes are used as weights in NURBS. This helps to increase the likelihood of the generated trajectory. The details about temporal trajectory modeling is discussed in Chapter 5.

In our framework, we can alternatively infer facial deformation dynamics from correlated signals, such as in speech-driven animation and visual face tracking. In that case, the facial deformation is inferred from input signals at every time instance. (See Chapter 4, Section 2 for visual tracking driven animation, and Chapter 5, Section 1.3 for speech-driven animation.) The mapping from related signal to facial deformation, however, can be many-to-many (as in speech-driven animation) or noisy (as in tracking). Thus, the proposed temporal model is still useful. We plan to incorporate dynamics model in speech-driven animation and visual face tracking in the future.

7.   Summary

In this chapter, a geometric 3D facial motion model is introduced. Compared to handcrafted models, the proposed model is derived from motion capture data so that it can capture the characteristics of real facial motions more easily. We have also discussed methods for applying the motion model to different subjects and face models with different topologies. The applications of the motion model in face analysis and synthesis will be presented in Chapter 4 and Chapter 5, respectively.

Chapter 4

GEOMETRIC MODEL-BASED 3D FACE TRACKING

To achieve robust 3D non-rigid face tracking, facial motion model is needed. In this chapter, we first review previous works on face tracking in Section 1. Next, in Section 2, we describe the geometric MU-based facial motion tracking algorithm. Section 3 will describe applications of our geometric 3D face tracking algorithm.

1. Previous Work

Analysis of human facial motion is the key component for many applications, such as model-based very low bit rate video coding for visual telecommunication [Aizawa and Huang, 1995], audio/visual speech recognition [Stork and Hennecke, 1996], expression recognition [Bartlett et al., 1999]. A large amount of work has been done on facial motion tracking. Simple approaches only utilize low-level image features. Although their computation complexity is low, they are not robust enough. For example, Goto et al. [Goto et al., 2001] extract edge information to find salient facial feature regions (e.g. eyes, lips, etc.). The extracted low-level image features are compared with templates to estimate the shapes of facial features. However, it is not robust enough to use low-level image features alone. The error will be accumulated with the increase in number of frames being tracked. High-level knowledge of facial deformation must be used to handle error accumulation problem by imposing constraints on the possible deformed facial shapes. It has been shown that robust tracking algorithm needs to integrate low-level image information and high-level knowledge. Examples of high-level constraints include: (1) parameterized geometric models such as B-Spline curves [Chan, 1999], snake model [Kass et al., 1988], deformable template [Yullie et al., 1992], and 3D parameterized model [DeCarlo, 1998]; (2) FACS-based models [Essa and Pentland, 1997, Tao and Huang, 1999]; and

(3) statistical shape and appearance models, such as ASM [Cootes et al., 1995] and AAM [Cootes et al., 1998].

1.1   Parameterized geometric models

1.1.1   B-Spline curves

Blake et al. [Blake et al., 1993] propose parametric B-spline curves for contour tracking. The tracking problem is to estimate the control points of the B-spline curve so that the B-spline curve matches the contour being tracked as closely as possible. However, without global constraints, B-spline curves tend to match contours locally, resulting in wrong matching among contour points. The robustness of the algorithm could be improved by employing constraints on the possible solution subspace of the contour points [Blake et al., 1995]. Therefore, it prevents generating physically impossible curves. Instead of using grey-level edge information, Kaucic and Blake [Kaucic and Blake, 1998] and Chan [Chan, 1999] utilize the characteristics of human skin color. They propose using either Bayesian classification or linear discriminant analysis to distinguish lips and other areas of facial skin. Therefore. the contours of the lips can be extracted more reliably. It is well known that color segmentation is sensitive to lighting conditions and the effectiveness of color segmentation depends on the subject. This can be partially solved by training a color classifier for each individual. Nevertheless, these two approaches do not handle 3D rotation, translation and appearance changes of lips.

1.1.2   Snake model

Kass et al. [Kass et al., 1988] propose the snake for tracking deformable contours. It starts from an initial starting point and deforms itself to match with the nearest salient contour. The matching procedure is formulated as an energy minimization process. In basic Snake-based tracking, the function to be minimized includes two energy terms: (1) internal spline energy caused by stretching and bending, and (2) measure of the attraction of image features such as contours. B-Spline [Blake et al., 1993] is a "least squares" style Snake algorithm. Snakes rely on gray-level gradient information for measuring the energy terms of the snakes. However, it is possible that gray-level gradients in images are inadequate for identifying the contour. Therefore, Terzopoulos and Waters [Terzopoulos and Waters, 1990a] highlighted the facial features by makeup to help Snake-based tracking. Otherwise, Snakes very often align onto undesirable local minima. To improve Snakes, Bregler and Konig [Bregler and Konig, 1994] propose *eigenlips* that incorporate a lip shape manifold into Snake tracker for lip tracking. The shape manifold is learned from training sequences of lip shapes. It imposes global constraints on the Snake contour shape model.

The local search for maximum gray-level gradients is guided by the globally learned lip shape space.

1.1.3 Deformable template

Yullie et al. [Yullie et al., 1992] define a facial feature as a deformable template, which includes a parametric geometrical model and an imaging model. Deformable template poses tracking as an analysis-by-synthesis problem. The geometrical model describes how the shape of the template can be deformed and is used to measure shape distance from the template. The imaging model describes how to generate an instance of the template and is used to measure the intensity distance from the template. An energy function is designed to link different types of low-level image features, such as intensity, peaks, and edges, to the corresponding properties of the template. The parameters of the template are calculated by steepest descent. Nonetheless, the parametric facial feature models are usually defined subjectively.

1.1.4 3D parameterized model

DeCarlo and Mataxas [DeCarlo and Metaxas, 2000] propose an approach that combines a deformable model space and multiple image cues (optical flow and edge information) to track facial motions. The edge information used is chosen around certain facial features, such as the boundary of the lips and eyes. To avoid high computation complexity, optical flow is calculated only for a set of image pixels. Those image pixels are chosen in the region covered by the face model using the method proposed by Shi and Tomasi [Shi and Tomasi, 1994]. The deformable model is a parametric geometric mesh model. The parameters are manually designed based on a set of anthropometric measurements of the face. By changing the values of the parameters, the user can obtain a different basic face shape and deform the basic face shape locally. The deformable model in [DeCarlo and Metaxas, 2000] helps to prevent producing unlikely facial shapes during tracking. However, it is labor-intensive to construct the face deformation model, and some facial deformation (e.g. lip deformations produced during speech) may not be represented adequately using the anthropometric measurements.

1.2 FACS-based models

A number of researchers have proposed to model facial deformation using FACS system. The FACS based 3D models impose constraints on the subspace of the plausible facial shapes. The motion parameters include global face motion parameters (rotation and translation) and local facial deformation parameters, which correspond to the weights of AUs in [Li et al., 1993, Tao and Huang, 1999] and to the FACS-like control parameters in [Essa and Pentland, 1997]. In these approaches, first, the movements of the vertices on the model are calculated using optical flow. The optical flow results are usually noisy. The facial deformation model is then added to constrain the noisy 2D image motion. The motion parameters are calculated by least square estimator. However, FACS was originally proposed for psychology study and does not provide quantitative information about facial deformations. To utilize FACS, researchers need to manually design the parameters of their model to obtain the AUs. This manual design process is usually labor-intensive. Li et al. [Li et al., 1993] uses a parametric geometrical face model, called Candide. The Candide model contains a set of parameters for controlling facial shape. Tao and Huang [Tao and Huang, 1999] use a piecewise Bezier volume deformable face model, which can be deformed by changing the coordinates of the control vertices of the Bezier volumes. In [Essa and Pentland, 1997], Essa and Pentland extended a mesh face model, which was developed by Platt and Badler [Platt and Badler, 1981], into a topologically invariant physics-based model by adding anatomy-based "muscles," which is defined by FACS.

1.3   Statistical models

1.3.1   Active Shape Model (ASM) and Active Appearance Model (AAM)

Active Shape model (ASM) [Cootes et al., 1995], Active Appearance model (AAM) [Cootes et al., 1998], utilize variations of both contour and appearance to model the facial motion. They are both analysis-by-synthesis approaches. ASM and AAM try to achieve robust performance by using the high-level model to constrain solutions to be valid examples of the object being tracked. The appearance of the object is explained by the high-level model as a compact set of model parameters. The models used by ASM and AAM are the eigen-features of the object. ASM models the shape variation of a set of landmark points and the texture variation in the local areas around landmark points. AAM models the contour and the appearance inside of the contour of the object. Both of them require manually labelled training data, which is labor intensive. The training data need to be carefully labelled so that the correspondences between the landmarks across training samples are physically correctly established. In order to handle various lighting conditions, the texture part of the training data should cover broad enough lighting conditions.

1.3.2   3D model learned from motion capture data

People have recently proposed to train facial motion subspace models from real facial motion data [Basu et al., 1998, Hong et al., 2001b, Kshirsagar et al., 2001, Reveret and Essa, 2001], which can capture the real motion characteristics of facial features better than manually defined models. The approaches presented in [Basu et al., 1998, Reveret and Essa, 2001] only deal with lips. The trained 3D model is able to encode the information of real lip deformations. Principal component analysis are used in [Hong et al., 2001b, Kshirsagar et al., 2001, Reveret and Essa, 2001] to derive basis of facial deformation model. Then the basis can be used for face animation [Hong et al., 2001b, Kshirsagar et al., 2001, Reveret and Essa, 2001] and tracking [Hong et al., 2001b].

2. Geometric MU-based 3D Face Tracking

In the conventional 3D non-rigid face tracking algorithm using FACS-based 3D facial deformation model, the subspace spanned by the Action Units (AUs) is used as the high-level knowledge to guide face tracking. Similar to MU, AUs are defined such that arbitrary facial deformation is approximated by a linear combination of AUs. However, the AUs are usually manually designed. For these approaches, our automatically learned MUs can be used in place of the manually designed AUs. In this way, extensive manual intervention can be avoided, and natural facial deformation can be approximated better.

We choose to use the learned MUs in the 3D non-rigid face tracking system proposed in [Tao and Huang, 1999], because the system has been shown to be: (1) robust in face of gradual background changes; (2) able to recover from temporary loss of tracking; and (3) real-time in tracking speed. For these reasons, this tracking system has been effectively used for bimodal speech recognition [Zhang et al., 2000] and emotion recognition [Cohen et al., 2003]. The facial motion observed in image plane can be represented by

$$\mathbf{M}(\mathbf{R}(\vec{V}_0 + \mathbf{L}\,\vec{P}) + \vec{T}) \tag{4.1}$$

where $\mathbf{M}$ is the projection matrix, $\vec{V}_0$ is the neutral face, $\mathbf{L}\,\vec{P}$ defines the non-rigid deformation, $\mathbf{R}$ is the 3D rotation decided by three rotation angles $[w_x, w_y, w_z]^t = \vec{W}$, and $\vec{T}$ stands for 3D translation. $\mathbf{L}$ is an $N \times M$ matrix that contains M AUs, each of which is an N dimensional vector. $\vec{P} = [p_1, ..., p_M]^t$ is the coefficients of the AUs. To estimate facial motion parameters $\{\vec{T}, \vec{W}, \vec{P}\}$ from 2D inter-frame motion $d\vec{V}_{2D}$, the derivative of equation 4.1 is taken with respect to $\{\vec{T}, \vec{W}, \vec{P}\}$. Then, a linear equation between $d\hat{V}_{2D}$ and $\{d\vec{T}, d\vec{W}, d\vec{P}\}$ can be derived by ignoring high order derivatives (see details in [Tao and Huang, 1999]). The system estimates $d\hat{V}_{2D}$ using template-matching-based optical flow. After that, the linear system is solved using least square in a multi-resolution manner for efficiency and robustness.

In the original system, $\mathbf{L}$ was manually designed using Bezier volume, and represented by the displacements of vertices of face surface mesh. The design process was labor-intensive. To derive $\mathbf{L}$ from the learned MUs in our current system, the "MU fitting" process described in Chapter 3 is used. For the adaptation, it requires that the face be in its neutral position in the first image frame and the facial feature locations are detected. In the original system, it is already done interactively via a GUI. In the future, we plan to detect these feature locations automatically such that the whole fitting could be automatic.

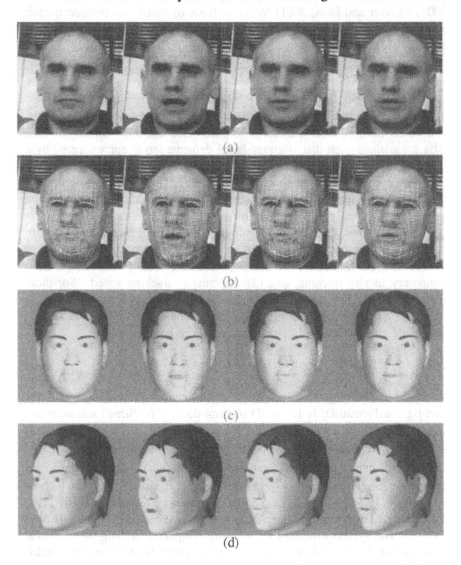

Figure 4.1. Typical tracked frames and corresponding animated face models. (a): The input image frames. (b): The tracking results visualized by yellow mesh overlayed on input images. (c): The front views of the face model animated using tracking results. (d): The side views of the face model animated using tracking results. In each row, the first image corresponds to neutral face.

In the current system, we use the holistic MUs derived in Section 3 of Chapter 3. Parts-based MUs could be used if a certain local region is the focus of interests, such as the lips in speech reading. The system is implemented in a PC with two 2.2 GHz *Pentium* 4 processors and 2GB memory. The image size of the input video is 640×480. With only one CPU employed, the system works at 14 frame/second for non-rigid face tracking. The tracking results can be visualized by using the coefficients of MUs, R and $\vec{T}$ to directly animate face models. Figure 4.1 shows some typical frames that it tracked, along with the animated face model to visualize the results. It can be observed that compared with neutral face (the first column images), the mouth opening (the second column), subtle mouth rounding and mouth protruding (the third and fourth columns) are captured in the tracking results visualized by animated face models.

3. Applications of Geometric 3D Face Tracking

The facial motion synthesis using tracking results can be used in model-based face video coding such as [Huang and Tao, 2001, Tu et al., 2003]. In our face video coding experiments [Tu et al., 2003], we track and encode the face area using model-based coding. To encode the residual in face area and the background for which a-priori knowledge is not generally available, we use traditional waveform-based coding method H.26L. This hybrid approach improves the robustness of the model-based method at the expense of increasing bit-rate. Eisert et al. [Eisert et al., 2000] proposed a similar hybrid coding technique using a different model-based 3D facial motion tracking approach. We capture and code videos of 352×240 at 30Hz. At the same low bit-rate (18 kbits/s), we compare this hybrid coding with H.26L JM 4.2 reference software. In Chapter 9, Figure 4.2 shows three snapshots of a video that we used in our experiment. This video has 147 frames. For the video used in our experiments, the Peak Signal to Noise Ratio (PSNR) around facial area for hybrid coding is 2dB higher compared to H.26L. Moreover, the hybrid coding results have much higher visual quality. Because our tracking system works in real-time, it could be used in a real-time low bit-rate video phone application. More details of the model-based face video coding application will be discussed in Chapter 9.

Besides low bit-rate video coding, the tracking results can used as the visual features for audio-visual speaker independent speech recognition [Zhang et al., 2000], and emotion recognition [Cohen et al., 2003]. The bimodal speech recognition system improves the speech recognition rate in noisy environments. The emotion recognition system is being used to monitor students' emotional and cognitive states in a computer-aided instruction application. In medical applications related to facial motion disorder such as facial paralysis, visual cues are important for both diagnosis and treatment. Therefore, the facial motion analysis method can be used as a diagnostic tool such as in [Wachtman et al.,

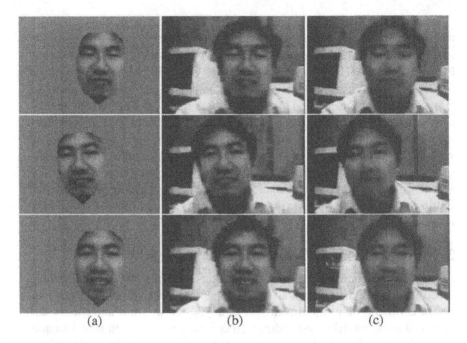

Figure 4.2. (a): The synthesized face motion. (b): The reconstructed video frame with synthesized face motion. (c): The reconstructed video frame using H.26L codec.

2001]. Compared to other 3D non-rigid facial motion tracking approaches using single camera, which are cited in Section 1, the features of our tracking system can be summarized as: (1) the deformation space is learned automatically from data such that it avoids manual crafting but still captures the characteristics of real facial motion; (2) it is real-time so that it can be used in real-time human computer interface and coding applications; (3) To reduce "drifting" caused by error accumulation in long-term tracking, it uses templates in both the initial frame and previous frame when estimating the template-matching-based optical flow (see [Tao and Huang, 1999]); and (4) it is able to recover from temporary loss of tracking by incorporating a template-matching-based face detection module.

4. Summary

In this chapter, a robust real-time 3D geometric face tracking system is presented. The proposed motion-capture-based geometric motion model is adopted in the tracking system to replace the original handcrafted facial motion model. Therefore, extensive manual editing of the motion model can be avoided. Using the estimated geometric motion parameters, we conduct experiments on video-driven face animation and very low bit-rate face animation. The experimental results show that geometric facial motions can be effectively captured in the tracking results. The presented tracking system can be used in many other HCI applications, such as facial expressions recognition, human behavior understanding, and etc.

Chapter 5

GEOMETRIC FACIAL MOTION SYNTHESIS

In this section, we discuss the facial motion synthesis using the trained Motion Unit model. Our goal is to use learned models to synthesize plausible facial appearance for providing visual cues in synthetic face based interactions. In Chapter 3, we have discussed that linear combinations of geometric MUs can be used to approximate arbitrary face shapes. In this chapter, we focus on how to produce animation according to various input signals, such as text and speech. We first review previous work on face animation in Section 1. Next, we introduce face motion trajectory for face animation in Section 2. After text-driven face animation and offline speech-driven animation are discussed in Section 3 and 4, respectively. Finally we describe real-time speech-driven animation in Section 5.

1. Previous Work

Based on spatial and temporal modeling of facial deformation, facial motion is usually synthesized according to semantic input, such as actor performance [Williams, 1990], text script [Waters and Levergood, 1993], or speech [Brand, 1999, Morishima and Yotsukura, 1999].

1.1 Performance-driven face animation

Performance-driven face animation animates face models according to visual input signals. This type of approach automatically analyzes real facial movements in the video using computer vision techniques. The analysis results are used to animate graphic face models. Williams [Williams, 1990] put markers on the subject's face and use simple tracking algorithm to estimate the motion of the markers. Guenter et al. [Guenter et al., 1998] put more markers on faces and track their 3D motion to achieve high quality visual input. However, both Williams [Williams, 1990] and Guenter et al. [Guenter et al., 1998] required intrusive markers be put on the face of the subject. This limits the conditions where there approaches can be used. Other approaches [Eisert et al., 2000, Essa and Pentland, 1997, Tao and Huang, 1999, Terzopoulos and Waters, 1990a] used more sophisticated facial motion analysis techniques to avoid using markers. The quality of the animation depends on the estimated facial motions. Therefore, the key issue is to achieve robust and accurate face motion estimation from noisy image motion. However, it is still a challenging problem to estimate facial motions accurately and robustly without using markers.

1.2   Text-driven face animation

Synthesizing facial motions during speech is useful in many applications, such as e-commerce [Pandzic et al., 1999], computer-aided education [Cole et al., 1999]. One type of input of this "visual speech" synthesis is text. First, the text is converted into a sequence of phonemes by *Text-To-Speech* (TTS) system. Then, the phoneme sequence is mapped to corresponding facial shapes, called visemes. Finally, a smooth temporal facial shape trajectory is synthesized considering the co-articulation effect in speech. It is combined with the synthesized audio-only speech signal from TTS as the final animation. Waters et al. [Waters and Levergood, 1993] and Hong et al. [Hong et al., 2001a] generated the temporal trajectory using sinusoidal interpolation functions. Pelachaud et al. [Pelachaud et al., 1991] used a look-ahead co-articulation model. Cohen and Massaro [Cohen and Massaro, 1993] adopted Löfqvist gestural production model [Lofqvist,] as the co-articulation model and interactively designed its explicit form based on observation of real speech.

1.3   Speech-driven face animation

Another type of input for "visual speech" synthesis   speech signals. For speech-driven face animation, the main research issue is the audio-to-visual mapping. The audio information is usually represented by acoustic features such as linear predictive coding (LPC) cepstrum, Mel-frequency cepstral coefficients (MFCC). The visual information is usually represented by the parameters of facial motion models, such as the weights of AU's, MPEG-4 FAPs, the coordinates of model control points etc. The mappings are learned from an audio-visual training data set, which are collected in the following way. The facial movements of talking subjects are tracked either manually or automatically. The tracking results and the associated audio tracks are collected as the audio-visual training data.

Some speech-driven face animation approaches use phonemes or words as intermediate representations. Lewis [Lewis, 1989] uses linear prediction to recognize phonemes. The recognized phonemes are associated with mouth positions to provide key frames for face animation. However, the phoneme recognition rate of linear prediction is low. Video Rewrite [Bregler et al., 1997] trains hidden Markov models (HMMs) [Rabiner, 1989] to automatically label phonemes in both training audio track and new audio track. It models short-term mouth co-articulation using triphones. The mouth images for a new audio track are generated by reordering the mouth images in the training footage, which requires a very large database. Video Rewrite is an offline approach and needs large computation resources. Chen and Rao [Chen and Rao, 1998] train HMMs to segment the audio feature vectors of isolated words into state sequences. Given the trained HMMs, the state probability for each time stamp is evaluated using the Viterbi algorithm. The estimated visual features of all states can be weighted by the corresponding probabilities to obtain the final visual features, which are used for lip animation. The advantage of using the intermediate representations is that people can make use of the knowledge about speech recognition and the phoneme-to-visual mapping in text-driven animation. The disadvantage is that it requires long enough context information to recognize phoneme or words so that it can not achieve real-time speech-driven face animation.

Another HMM-based approach tries to directly map audio patterns to facial motion trajectories. Voice Puppetry [Brand, 1999] uses an entropy minimization algorithm to train HMMs for the audio to visual mapping. The mapping estimates a probability distribution over the manifold of possible facial motions from the audio stream. An advantage of this approach is that it does not require automatically recognizing speech into high-level meaningful symbols (e.g., phonemes, words), which is very difficult to obtain a high recognition rate. Nevertheless, this approach is an offline method.

Other approaches attempt to generate instantaneous lip shapes directly from each audio frame using vector quantization, Gaussian mixture model, or artificial neural networks (ANN). Vector quantization-based approach [Morishima et al., 1989] classifies the audio features into one of a number of classes. Each class is then mapped onto a corresponding visual output. Though it is computationally efficient, the vector quantization approach often leads to discontinuous mapping results. The Gaussian mixture approach [Rao and Chen, 1996] models the joint probability distribution of the audio-visual vectors as a Gaussian mixture. Each Gaussian mixture component generates an optimal estimation for a visual feature given an audio feature. The estimations are then nonlinearly weighted to produce the final visual estimation. The Gaussian mixture approach produces smoother results than the vector quantization approach. However, neither of these two approach described consider phonetic context information, which is very important for modeling mouth coarticulation during speech. Neural network based approaches try to find nonlinear audio-to-visual mappings. Morishima and Harashima [Morishima and Harashima, 1991] trained a three layer neural network to map LPC Cepstrum speech coefficients of one time step speech signals to mouth-shape parameters for five vowels. Kshirsagar and Magnenat-Thalmann [Kshirsagar and Magnenat-Thalmann, 2000] also trained a three-layer neural network to classify speech segments into vowels. Nonetheless, these two approaches do not consider phonetic context information. In addition, they mainly consider the mouth shapes of vowels and neglect the contribution of consonants during speech. Massaro et al. [Massaro and et al., 1999] trained multilayer perceptrons (MLP) to map LPC cepstral parameters to face animation parameters. They try to model the coarticulation by considering the speech context information of five backward and five forward time windows. Another way to model speech context information is to use time delay neural networks (TDNNs) model to perform temporal processing. Lavagetto [Lavagetto, 1995] and Curinga et al. [Curinga et al., 1996] trained TDNN to map LPC cepstral coefficients of speech signal to lip animation parameters. TDNN is chosen because it can model the temporal coarticulation of lips. These artificial neural networks, however, require a large number of hidden units, which results in high computational complexity during the training phrase. Vignoli et al. [Vignoli et al., 1996] used self-organizing maps (SOM) as a classifier to perform vector quantization functions and fed the classification results to a TDNN. SOM reduces the dimension of input of TDNN so that it reduces the parameters of TDNN. However, the recognition results of SOM are discontinuous which may affect the final output.

2. Facial Motion Trajectory Synthesize

In iFACE system, text-driven and off-line driven speech-driven animation are synthesized using phoneme sequences, generated by text-to-speech module or audio alignment tool. Each phoneme p corresponds to a key shape, or a control point the dynamics model in our framework. Each phoneme is modeled as a multidimensional Gaussian with mean μ_p and covariance Σ_p.

A phoneme sequence constrains the temporal trajectory of facial motion at certain time instances. To generate a smooth trajectory given these constraints, we use NURBS (Nonuniform Rational B-splines) interpolation. The NURBS trajectory is defined as:

$$C(t) = \frac{\sum_{i=0}^{n} N_{i,p}(t) \, w_i \, P_i}{\sum_{i=0}^{n} N_{i,p}(t) \, w_i} \qquad (5.1)$$

where p is the order of the NURBS, $N_{i,p}$ is the basis function, P_i is control point of the NURBS, and w_i is the weight of P_i. Usually people use $p = 2$ or $p = 3$. In our framework, we use $p = 2$. The phonemes (key facial configurations) are used as control points, which we assume to have Gaussian distributions (the method can be trivially generalized to Gaussian mixtures). The derivation of the phoneme model is discussed in Section 3. We set the weight of each control point such that the trajectory has higher likelihood. Intuitively, it can be achieved in a way that states with small variance pull the trajectory towards them, while states with larger variance allow the trajectory to stay way from them. Therefore we set the weights to be $w_i = 1/(\sigma(\vec{n}_i))$, where $\vec{n}_i$ is the trajectory normal vector that also passes $\mathbf{P}_i$, $\sigma(\vec{n}_i)$ is the variance of the Gaussian distribution in $\vec{n}_i$ direction. In practice, it is not trivial to compute $\vec{n}_i$. Thus, we approximate it by normal vector $\vec{n}'_i$ of line segment $\overline{\mathbf{P}_{i-1}\mathbf{P}_{i+1}}$ (see $\overline{\mathbf{P}_1\mathbf{P}_3}$ in Figure 5.1(a)). Compared to [Brand, 1999], the smooth trajectory obtained is less optimal in terms of maximum likelihood. But it is fast and robust, especially when the number of states is small or the assumed HMM topology fits the data poorly. Ezzat et al. [Ezzat et al., 2002] propose an trajectory synthesis approach similar in spirit to ours. But our formulation is easier in a sense that it can viewed as a natural extension of traditional key-frame-based spline interpolation scheme, given the probability distribution of each key frame. Figure 5.1 shows a synthetic example comparing conventional NURBS and our statistically weighted NURBS. The dots are samples of facial shapes.

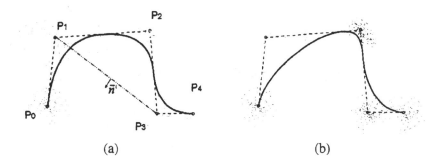

Figure 5.1. (a): Conventional NURBS interpolation. (b): Statistically weighted NURBS interpolation.

The dashed line connects centers of the states. The solid line is the generated facial deformation trajectory. In Figure 5.1(b), the trajectory is pulled towards the states with smaller variance, thus have higher likelihood than trajectory in Figure 5.1(a). Ezzat et al. [Ezzat et al., 2002] observed that the generated trajectory by spline-based method could be "under-articulated". To reduce the undesirable effect, they proposed to adjust the center and variance of the Gaussian model based on training data. We plan to perform similar adjustments in our framework.

3.   Text-driven Face Animation

When text is used in communication, e.g., in the context of text-based electronic chatting over the Internet or visual email, visual speech synthesized from
text will greatly help deliver information. Recent work on text driven face animation includes the work of Cohen and Massaro [Cohen and Massaro, 1993],
Ezzat and Poggio [Ezzat and Poggio, 2000] , and Waters and Levergood [Waters
and Levergood, 1993].

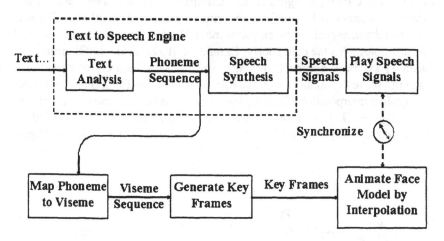

Figure 5.2.   The architecture of text driven talking face.

Similar to the work of Ezzat and Poggio [Ezzat and Poggio, 2000] and that
of Waters and Levergood [Waters and Levergood, 1993], our framework adopts
the key frame based face animation technique for text-driven face animation.
The procedure of the text driven face animation is illustrated in Figure 5.2.
Our framework uses Microsoft Text-to-Speech (TTS) engine for text analysis
and speech synthesis. First, the text stream is fed into the TTS engine. TTS
parses the text and generates the corresponding phoneme sequence, the timing
information of phonemes, and the synthesized speech stream. Each phoneme
is mapped to a viseme based on a lookup table. Each viseme is a key frame.
Therefore, the text is translated in to a key frame sequence. A temporal trajectory is then synthesized based on the key frame sequence using the technique
described in Section 2.

In the framework, we use a label system that has forty-four phonemes. Sev-
enteen viseme groups are design to group visually similar phonemes together.
The phonemes and their viseme group labels are shown in Table 5.1.

In our experiment, we use the motion capture data in Chapter 3 to train the
key shape model for each viseme. Each shape is represented using MUPs,

Phoneme	Word	Viseme label	Phoneme	Word	Viseme label
SIL	Silence	17	HX	*head*	8
IY	*beat*	10	M	*meet*	1
IH	*bit*	8	N	*net*	5
EY	*bait*	8	NX	si*ng*	8
EH	*bet*	8	EL	bott*le*	11
AE	*bat*	13	D	*debt*	5
AA	*pot*	14	EN	butt*on*	5
AY	*buy*	8	F	*f*in	2
AW	*down*	8	V	*vet*	2
AH	*but*	8	TH	*th*in	3
AO	*bought*	15	DH	*th*is	3
OW	*boat*	16	S	*sit*	5
OY	*boy*	5	Z	*z*oo	5
UH	*book*	7	SH	*sh*oe	4
UW	*lute*	6	ZH	mea*s*ure	4
YU	*cute*	12	P	*pet*	1
AX	*about*	7	B	*bet*	1
IX	kiss*es*	5	T	*test*	5
W	*wet*	6	G	*get*	5
Y	*yet*	5	K	*kit*	5
R	*red*	9	CH	*ch*urch	4
LL	*let*	11	JH	*j*udge	4

Table 5.1. Phoneme and viseme used in face animation.

which are modeled using a Gaussian model. Each key shape has a mean shape and a covariance matrix. The key shape viseme models are then used in the key-frame-based face animation, such as text-driven animation. Four of the key shapes and the largest components of their variances are shown in Figure 5.3. They correspond to phonemes: (a) M; (b) AA; (c) UH; and (d) EN. Because we only use the relative ratio of the variance values, we normalize variance values to be in the range [0, 1].

4. Offline Speech-driven Face Animation

When human speech is used in one-way communication, e.g. news broadcasting over the networks, using real speech in face animation is better than using synthetic speech. Because the communication is one-way, the audio-to-visual mapping can be done offline, i.e. the animation can come out until the end of a batch of speech. The process of offline speech driven face animation is illustrated in Figure 5.4. An advantage of offline process is that the phoneme transcription and timing information can be extracted accurately for animation purpose, given the text script of the speech. Recognizing phoneme

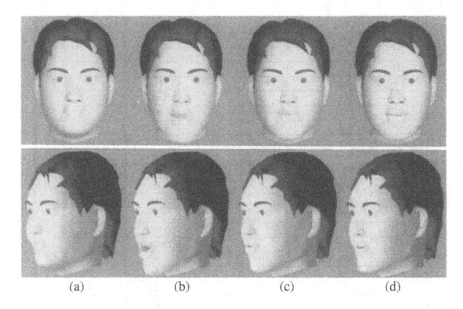

Figure 5.3. Four of the key shapes. The top row images are front views and the bottom row images are the side views. The largest components of variances are (a): 0.67; (b): 1.0;, (c): 0.18; (d): 0.19.

using only speech signals requires a complicated continuous speech recognizer, and the phoneme recognition rate and the timing information may not be accurate enough. The text script associated with speech, however, provides the accurate word-level transcription so that it greatly simplifies the complexity and also improves the accuracy. We use a phoneme speech alignment tool, which comes with Hidden Markov Model Toolkit (HTK) 2.0 [HTK, 2004] for phoneme recognition and alignment. Speech stream is decoded into phoneme sequence with timing information. Once we have the phoneme sequence and the timing information, the remaining part of the procedure of the visual speech synthesis is similar to text driven face animation.

5.   Real-time Speech-driven Face Animation

Real-time speech-driven face animation is demanded for real-time two-way communications such as teleconferencing. The key issue is to derive the real-time audio-to-visual mapping. In Section 5.1, we describe a formant-analysis-based feature for real-time speech animation. Then we present a real-time audio-to-visual mapping based on artificial neural network (ANN) in Section 5.2.

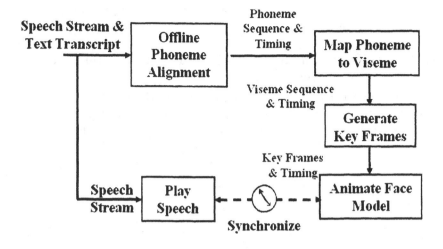

Figure 5.4. The architecture of offline speech driven talking face.

5.1 Formant features for real-time speech-driven face animation

Multiple acoustic features are correlated to vocal tract shape. LPC features are one of the most widely used features for speech driven animation [Brand, 1999, Curinga et al., 1996, Morishima and Yotsukura, 1999]. In this section, we describe a technique using formant frequencies as acoustic features because it is directly related to vowel-like sound including vowels, diphthongs and semivowels. It is observed that the vowel sounds account for major shapes of the mouth and make major contributions to the movement of mouth. Thus formant analysis enables us to build a simple yet effective mapping for speech driven animation [Wen et al., 2001].

5.1.1 Formant analysis

Human speech production system consists of two main components, the vocal cords and the vocal tract. The vocal cords excitation serves as the source of signal while vocal tract acts as a time-variant filter. The characteristics of the two components decide the final output speech. In speech production, the resonance frequencies of the vocal tract tube are called formant frequencies or simply formants. The formant frequencies depend on the shape of vocal tract and each shape is characterized by a set of formants [Rabiner and Shafer, 1978]. In practice, formant analysis is widely used to extract vocal tract characteristics for speech analysis and synthesis. Many methods are available for formants estimation. In our system, we use a method based on LPC parameters [Rabiner and Shafer, 1978]. First, we compute LPC coefficients, then find the roots of the linear predictor polynomial and choose formants from the roots.

5.1.2   An efficient real-time speech-driven animation system based on formant analysis

We have shown the effectiveness of formant features in speech-driven animation in a real-time system. The architecture of the system is shown in Figure 5.5. The close relationship of formant features and vowel-like sounds has enabled

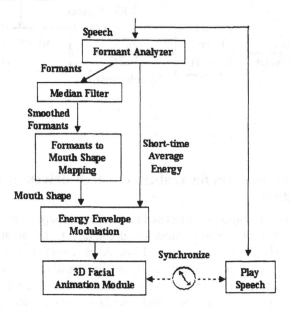

Figure 5.5.   The architecture of a real-time speech-driven animation system based on formant analysis.

a reasonably good linear audio-to-visual mapping. Ideally, if we assume a one-to-one mapping from formants to vocal tract shape, a direct one-to-one mapping from formants to mouth shape can be derived since mouth is part of vocal tract. In practice that assumption doesn't hold because variability and uncertainty is introduced by many factors in speech production. For example, estimated formants of unvoiced speech generally cannot give a correct description of the vocal tract shape. Different speakers have different formants for the same mouth shape due to the differences of the internal vocal tract. Fortunately, research has shown that the direct mapping can be approximated for vowel-like sounds. From research that has been done to measure the formant frequencies of vowel-like sounds, it is known that the first two formant frequencies of vowels cluster in a stable triangular subspace ("vowel triangle"). For each vowel the formants are in a certain region distinguishable form other vowels. Along a smooth trajectory in the so called "vowel triangle" (Figure 5.6), the mouth shape changes smoothly. For other vowel-like sounds, diphthongs can

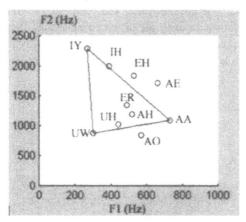

Figure 5.6. "Vowel Triangle" in the system, circles correspond to vowels [Rabiner and Shafer, 1978].

be modeled as transitions between vowels; semivowels are transitions between vowels and adjacent phonemes. Thus, they are (or partly are in the case of semivowels) trajectories in the ""vowel triangle" [Rabiner and Shafer, 1978]. Based on those facts, we can define mouth shapes corresponding to vowel-like sounds as a manifold over the "vowel triangle". The manifold could be learned from audio/visual data of recorded human speech. In our approach, we choose to take a much simpler alternative, which makes use of the phoneme-viseme correspondence. Visemes of vowels, which are widely used for facial anima-tion, can be seen as observations of the manifold. The mouth shapes in other places of the manifold can then be approximated by some interpolation tech-niques. In speaker-independent case, the "vowel triangle" is enlarged and there is overlap between different vowel regions [Rabiner and Shafer, 1978]. But much of a vowel region is still distinguishable from others so that each region can be roughly related to a unique mouth shape. Thus we can expect that the mouth shape manifold assumption can still produce reasonable mouth shapes, although less natural than the speaker-dependent case. In our system, we use the averaged values of measured formant frequencies of vowels for a wide range of talkers [Rabiner and Shafer, 1978]. For sounds other than vowel-like sounds, the proposed mapping is inadequate. Energy envelope modulation is used as a heuristics, to deal with that problem in the system shown in Figure 5.5 .

In the implemented real-time system, the average delay between speech input frame and the generated animation frame is less than 100 ms. The generated animation is then rendered synchronously with speech playback. The speech input and animation playback can run on different PCs via network, with only speech transmitted. To evaluate the effectiveness of our direct mapping method, we measure the motions of five points in mouth area synthesized by the direct mapping method, and compare them with the synthetic motion by text driven method. Figure 5.7 shows an example of the comparison. It can be observed that the speech driven method produces results comparable to the results of text driven method, which is widely used to generate facial animation.

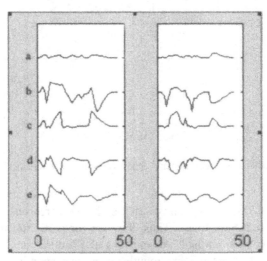

a: Motion of middle point of upper lip
b: Motion of middle point of lower lip
c: Motion of left corner of lip
d: Motion of right corner of lip
e: Motion of jaw

Figure 5.7. Comparison of synthetic motions. The left figure is text driven animation and the right figure is speech driven animation. Horizontal axis is the number of frames; vertical axis is the intensity of motion.

This system, though simple and effective for vowel-like sounds, is inadequate for unvoiced speech, and co-articulation is not well taken care of. Nonetheless, it shows the effectiveness of formant features for real-time speech driven animation. Next, we describe a more comprehensive real-time speech-driven animation system based on artificial neural network (ANN) in Section 5.2.

5.2 ANN-based real-time speech-driven face animation

In this section, we present our real-time speech-driven 3D face animation algorithm, as an animation example based on MUs in our 3D face analysis and synthesis framework. In this section, we propose a local non-linear audio-to-visual mapping based on ANN. We first classify audio features into groups. Then for each group we train an ANN for audio-to-visual mapping. In this way, the mapping can be more robust and accurate than simple classification based methods, such as VQ [Morishima et al., 1989] and GMM [Rao and Chen, 1996]. Our multi-ANN-based mapping is also more efficient in training than methods using only a single ANN [Morishima and Yotsukura, 1999, Kshirsagar and Magnenat-Thalmann, 2000, Massaro and et al., 19__, Lavagetto, 1995].

5.2.1 Training data and features extraction

We use the facial motion capture database (described in Section 2 of Chapter 3) along with its audio track for learning audio-to-visual mapping. To reduce the complexity of learning and make it more robust, the visual feature space should be small. Thus for this specific application we use the holistic MUs (Section 3 of Chapter 3) as the visual representation. For each 33 ms short time window, we calculate MUPs as the visual features and calculate twelve Mel-frequency cepstrum coefficients (MFCCs) [Rabiner and Juang, 1993] as the audio features. The audio feature vectors of frames $t - 3, t - 2, t - 1, t,$ $t + 1, t + 2,$ and $t + 3$, are concatenated in the temporal order as the final audio feature vector of frame t. Consequently, the audio feature vector of each audio frame has eighty-four elements. The frames $t - 3, t - 2, t - 1, t + 1, t + 2,$ and $t + 3$ define the contextual information of the frame t.

5.2.2 Audio-to-visual mapping

We modify the approaches that train neural networks as the audio-to-visual mapping [Hong et al., 2001b, Morishima and Yotsukura, 1999, Massaro and et al., 1999]. The training audio-visual data is divided into twenty-one groups based on the audio feature of each data sample. The number twenty-one is decided heuristically based on audio feature distribution of the training database. Particularly, one of the groups corresponds to silence because human beings are very sensitive to mouth movements if there is no sound generated. Other twenty groups are automatic generated using the k-mea_ _lgorithm. Then, the audio features of each group are modelled by a Gaussian model. After that, a three-layer perceptron is trained to map the audio features to the visual features using each audio-visual data group. At the estimation phase, we first classify an audio vector into one of the audio feature groups whose Gaussian model gives the highest score for the audio feature vector. We then select the corresponding neural network to map the audio feature vector to MUPs, which can be used in equation 3.1 to synthesize the facial shape. A method using triangular average window is used to smooth the jerky mapping results.

For each group, eighty percent of the data is randomly selected for training. The remaining data is used for testing. The maximum number of the hidden neurons is ten. The minimum number of the hidden neurons is four. A typical estimation result is shown in Figure 5.8. The horizontal axes in the figure represent time. The vertical axes represent the magnitude of the MUPs. The solid trajectory is the original MUPs, and the dashed trajectory is the estimation results.

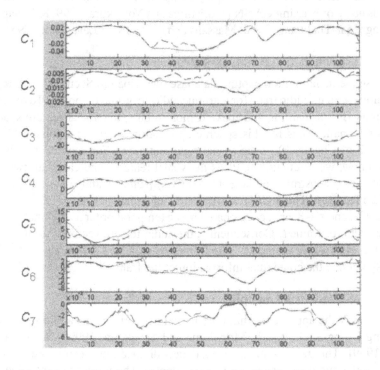

Figure 5.8.   Compare the estimated MUPs with the original MUPs. The content of the corresponding speech track is "A bird flew on lighthearted wing."

We reconstruct the facial deformation using the estimated MUPs and MUs. For both the ground truth and the estimated results, we divide the deformation of each facial feature point by its maximum absolute displacement in the ground truth data so that the magnitude of deformation is normalized to [-1.0, 1.0]. To evaluate the performance, we calculate the Pearson product-moment correlation coefficients (R) and the mean square error (MSE) using the normalized deformations. The Pearson product-moment correlation ($0.0 \leq R \leq 1.0$) measures how good the global match is between the shapes of two signal sequences. The larger the Pearson correlation coefficient, the better the estimated signal sequence matches with the original signal sequence.

The Pearson product-moment correlation coefficient R between the ground truth $\{\vec{d}_n\}$ and the estimated data $\{\vec{d}_n^l\}$ is calculated by

$$R = \frac{tr(E[(\vec{d}_n - \vec{\mu}_1)(\vec{d}_n^l - \vec{\mu}_2)^T])}{\sqrt{tr(E[(\vec{d}_n - \vec{\mu}_1)(\vec{d}_n - \vec{\mu}_1)^T])\,tr(E[(\vec{d}_n^l - \vec{\mu}_2)(\vec{d}_n^l - \vec{\mu}_2)^T])}} \tag{5.2}$$

where $\vec{\mu}_1 = E[\vec{d}_n]$ and $\vec{\mu}_2 = E[\vec{d}_n^l]$. In our experiment, R = 0.952 and MSE = 0.0069 for training data, and R = 0.946 and MSE = 0.0075 for testing data.

5.2.3   Animation result

The whole speech-driven 3D face animation procedure contains three steps. First, we extract audio features from the input speech stream, as described in Section 5.2.1. Then, we use the trained neural networks to map the audio features of an audio frame into the visual features (i.e. MUPs). Finally, we use the estimated MUPs to animate a personalized 3D face model in iFACE, to which the MUs have been adapted using methods described in Section 5 of Chapter 3. A typical animation sequence is presented in Figure 5.9.

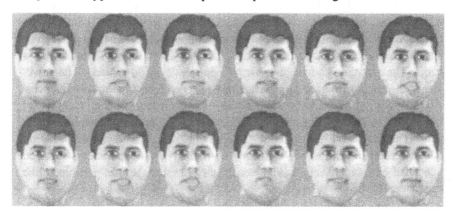

Figure 5.9.   Typical frames of the animation sequence of "A bird flew on lighthearted wing." The temporal order is from left to right, and from top to bottom.

Our real-time speech driven animation can be used in real-time two-way communication scenarios such as videophone, immersive conferencing in virtual environments [Leung et al., 2000]. On the other hand, existing off-line speech driven animation (e.g. "voice puppetry" [Brand, 1999]) can be used in one-way communication scenarios, such as broadcasting, advertising. Our approach deals the mapping of both vowels and consonants, thus it is more accurate than real-time approaches with only vowel-mapping [Kshirsagar and Magnenat-Thalmann, 2000, Morishima and Yotsukura, 1999]. Compared to real-time approaches using only one neural network for all audio features [Lavagetto, 1995, Massaro and et al., 1999], our local ANN mapping (i.e. one neural network for each audio feature cluster) is more efficient because each ANN is much simpler. Therefore it can be trained with much less effort for a certain set of training data. More generally, speech driven animation can be used in speech and language eduction [Cole et al., 1999], speech understanding aid for noisy environment and hard-of-hearing people, rehabilitation tool for facial motion disorders treatment.

5.2.4   Human emotion perception study

The synthetic talking face, which is used to convey visual cues to human, can be evaluated by human perception study. Here, we describe our experiments which compare the influence of the synthetic talking face on human emotion perception with that of the real face. We did similar experiments for 2D MU-based speech driven animation [Hong et al., 2002]. The experimental results can help the user with how to use the synthetic talking face to deliver the intended visual information.

We videotape a speaking subject who is asked to calmly read three sentences with 3 facial expressions: (1) neutral, (2) smile, and (3) sad, respectively. Hence, the audio tracks do not convey any emotional information. The contents of the three sentence are: (1) "It is normal."; (2) "It is good."; and (3) "It is bad.". The associated information is: (1) neutral; (2) positive; and (3) negative. The audio tracks are used to generate three sets of face animation sequences. All three audio tracks are used in each set of animation sequence. The first set is generated without expression. The second set is generated with smile expression. The third set is generated with sad expression. The facial deformation due to speech and expression is linearly combined in our experiments. Sixteen untrained human subjects, who never used our system before, participate the experiments.

The first experiment investigates human emotion perception based on either the visual stimuli alone or the audio stimuli alone. The subjects are first asked to recognize the expressions of both the real face and the synthetic talking face and infer their emotional states based on the animation sequences without audio. All subjects correctly recognized the expressions of both the synthetic face and the real face. Therefore, our synthetic talking face is capable to accurately deliver facial expression information. The emotional inference results in terms of the number of the subjects are shown in Table 5.2.   The "S" columns in Table 5.2, as well as in Table 5.4, 5.5, and 5.6, show the results using the synthetic talking face. The "R" columns show the results using the real face. As shown, the effectiveness of the synthetic talking face is comparable with that of the real face. The subjects are then asked to listen to the audio and decide the emotional state of the speaker. Each subject listens to each audio only once.

		Facial Expressions					
		Neutral		Smile		Sad	
		S	R	S	R	S	R
	Neutral	16	16	4	3	2	0
Emotion	Happy	0	0	12	13	0	0
	Sad	0	0	0	0	14	16

Table 5.2. Emotion inference based on video without audio track.

		Audio 1	Audio 2	Audio 3
	Neutral	16	6	7
Emotion	Happy	0	10	0
	Sad	0	0	9

Table 5.3. Emotion inference based on audio track.

		Facial Expressions					
		Neutral		Smile		Sad	
		S	R	S	R	S	R
	Neutral	16	16	2	1	1	0
Emotion	Happy	0	0	14	15	?	0
	Sad	0	0	0	0	15	16

Table 5.4. Emotion inference based on video with audio track 1.

Note that the audio tracks are produced without emotions. The results in terms of the number of the subjects are shown in Table 5.3.

The second and third experiments are designed to compare the influence of synthetic face on bimodal human emotion perception and that of the real face. In the second experiment, the subjects are asked to infer the emotional state while observing the synthetic talking face and listening to the audio tracks. In the third experiment, the subjects are asked to infer the emotional state while observing the real face and listening to the same audio tracks. We divide the subjects into two groups. Each of them has eight subjects. One group first participates the second experiment and then participates the third experiment. The other group first participates the third experiment and then participates the second experiment. The results are then combined and compared in Table 5.4, 5.5, and 5.6.

		Facial Expressions					
		Neutral		Smile		Sad	
		S	R	S	R	S	R
Emotion	Neutral	14	15	1	0	0	0
	Happy	2	1	15	16	0	0
	Sad	0	0	0	0	10	12
	Not sure	0	0	0	0	6	4

Table 5.5.   Emotion inference based on video with audio track 2.

		Facial Expressions					
		Neutral		Smile		Sad	
		S	R	S	R	S	R
Emotion	Neutral	11	13	10	11	0	0
	Happy	0	0	2	2	0	0
	Sad	5	3	0	0	16	16
	Not sure	0	0	4	3	0	0

Table 5.6.   Emotion inference based on video with audio track 3.

We can see the face movements (either synthetic or real) and the content of the audio tracks jointly influence the decisions of the subjects. Let us take the first audio track as an example (see Table 5.4). Although the first audio track only contains neutral information, fourteen subjects think the emotional state is happy if the expression of the synthetic talking face is smile. If the expression of the synthetic face is sad, fifteen subjects classify the emotional state into sad.

If the audio tracks and the facial represent the same kind of information, the human perception on the information is enhanced. For example, when the associated facial expression of the audio track 2 is smile, nearly all subjects say that the emotional state is happy (see Table 5.5). The numbers of the subjects who agree with happy emotion are higher than those using visual stimuli alone (see Table 5.2) or audio information alone (see Table 5.3).

However, it confuses human subjects if the facial expressions and the audio tracks represent opposite information. For example, many subjects are confused when they listen to an audio track with positive information, and observe a negative facial expression. An example is shown in the seventh and eighth columns of Table 5.5. The audio track conveys positive information while the facial expression is sad. Six subjects report that they are confused if the synthetic talking face with sad expression is shown. The number of the confused subjects reduces to four if the real face is used. This difference is mainly due to the fact that the subjects tend to trust real face more than synthetic face when confusion happens. Therefore, when the visual information conflicts with the audio information, the synthetic face is less capable of conveying fake emotion information.

Overall, the experimental results show that our real-time speech-driven synthetic talking face successfully affects human emotion perception. The effectiveness of the synthetic face is comparable with that of the real face though it is slightly weaker.

6. Summary

In this chapter, we present face animation methods based on geometric motion model. We describe three types of animation: text-driven, offline speech-driven and real-time speech-driven face animation. In all of the scenarios, our proposed geometric facial motion model serves as a compact and effective representation of visual information. A human perception study is conducted to demonstrate that the effectiveness of our synthetic face animation in conveying emotional cues.

Chapter 6

FLEXIBLE APPEARANCE MODEL

In previous chapters we have presented the geometric facial motion model, and how the model can be used in facial motion analysis and synthesis. Geometric motion model handles the macro- and meso-structure level deformations. However, facial motions also exhibit detailed appearance changes such as wrinkles and creases as well. These details are important visual cues for both human perception and computer analysis. Nevertheless, they are difficult to analyze and synthesize using geometric motion models. In this chapter, we introduce our flexible appearance model in our 3D face processing framework. It aims to deal with facial motion details, thus enhance the geometric model based analysis and synthesis. However, the space of all face appearance is huge, affected by the variations across different head poses, individuals, lighting, expressions, speech and etc. Thus it is difficult for most existing appearance-based methods to collect enough face appearance data and train a model that works robustly in many different scenarios. Compared to these approacnes, the novelty of our flexible appearance model is that we propose efficient and effective methods to reduce illumination dependency and person dependency of the appearance model, based on limited data. Therefore, it is more flexible to use the appearance model in varying conditions.

In Section 1, we first give a review of the related works on utilizing appearance models for facial motion analysis and synthesis. Then we introduce our flexible appearance model in Section 2. Section 2.1 describes the illumination modeling component of the flexible appearance model. Then, we discuss the technique for reducing person dependency in Section 2.2. Analysis and synthesis using the flexible model will be presented later in Chapter 7 and 8, respectively.

1.   Previous Work

1.1   Appearance-based facial motion modeling, analysis and synthesis

To capture the facial appearance changes not modeled by geometric models. appearance-based approaches use all face image pixel in analysis and synthesis. To reduce the high dimensionality of the appearance space the image samples are usually aligned first to remove the variation caused by global transformation. This alignment is mostly done manually or semi-automatically. Then, subspace analysis techniques such as Principal Component Analysis (PCA) [Jolliffe, 1986], are used to find low dimensional approximation of the space.

In appearance-based facial motion analysis, Bregler and Konig [Bregler and Konig, 1994] used PCA to learn "eigen lips" for bi-modal speech recognition. Besides PCA, the dimensionality of appearance space can be also reduced by extracting other texture-based features, such as Gabor wavelets coefficients [Donato et al., 1999]. To enhance certain features (e.g., edges), face images can be processed by filtering before extracting appearance-based features. These appearance-based features have been shown [Bartlett et al., 1999, Donato et al., 1999] to improve the recognition of AU's which incur detailed facial motion.

Beymer et al. [Beymer and Poggio, 1996] proposed to learn the nonlinear mapping between face appearance and its "parameters" (e.g. "pose", "expression") using multidimensional interpolation networks. The mappings could be learned in both direction: (1) from appearance to parameters; and (2) from parameters to appearance. Therefore the framework could be used for both analysis and synthesis. Ezzat et al. [Ezzat et al., 2002] extended the idea of "multidimensional interpolation" to visual speech synthesis. Cosatto and Graf [Cosatto and Graf, 2000] generated text-driven animation by finding smooth trajectories in extensive samples based on phonemes.

However, the space of all face appearance is huge, affected by the variations across different head poses, individuals, lighting, expressions, speech and etc. Thus it is difficult for appearance-based methods to collect enough face appearance data and train a model that works robustly in many different scenarios. In this respect, the geometric-based methods are more robust to large head motions, changes of lighting and are less person-dependent.

1.2   Hybrid facial motion modeling, analysis and synthesis

To combine the advantages of both approaches, people have been investigating methods of using both geometry (shape) and appearance (texture) in face analysis and synthesis. Guenter et al. [Guenter et al., 1998] captured both shape and texture using markers in performance-driven face animation. La Cascia et al. [Cascia et al., 2000] modeled the face with a texture-mapped cylinder. 3D rigid face tracking was formulated as a texture image registration problem. The Active Appearance Model (AAM) [Cootes et al., 1998] and its variants, apply PCA to model both the shape variations of image patches and their texture variations. They have been shown to be powerful tools for face alignment, recognition, and synthesis. Blanz and Vetter [Blanz and Vetter, 1999] proposed 3D morphable models for 3D faces modeling, which model the variations of both 3D face shape and texture using PCA. The 3D morphable models have been shown effective in 3D face animation and face recognition from non-frontal views [Blanz et al., 2002]. Pighin et an [Pighin et al., 1999] and Revert et al. [Reveret and Essa, 2001] estimated facial deformation based on the discrepancy between a target face image and the image synthesized from reference face texture images. Arbitrary facial shapes were approximated by a linear combination of a set of basic shapes. Furthermore, a linear combination of a set of reference texture images was used to cope with the texture variations. However, the set of reference texture images should be similar to the target face image, for example, same person, same lighting. Moreover, they were computationally expensive because all image pixels are used in the nonlinear Levenberg-Marquaardt optimization. Recently, Liu et al. [Liu et al., 2001a] applied both geometric and textural changes to synthesize realistic facial expressions. The ratio image technique was used to capture the subtle appearance changes independent of the face surface albedo. In facial expression classification, Tian et al. [Tian et al., 2002] and Zhang et al. [Zhang et al., 1998] proposed to train classifiers (e.g. neural networks) using both shape and texture features. The trained classifiers were shown to outperform classifiers using shape or texture features only.

In these hybrid approaches, some variations of texture are absorbed by shape variation models. However, the potential texture space can still be huge because many other variations are not modeled by the shape model. Moreover, little has been done to adapt the learned models to new conditions. As a result, the application of these methods are limited to conditions similar to those of training data.

1.3   Issues in flexible appearance model

Because the appearance of facial motions has large variations due to many factors, such poses, people and lighting conditions, it has been a difficult problem to adapt appearance models of facials motions to various conditions. In our framework, we focus on (1) the appearance model adaptation for synthesis over different illumination and people's face albedo; and (2) online appearance model adaptation during facial motion analysis.

1.3.1   Illumination effects of face appearance

The analysis and synthesis of human faces under arbitrary lighting conditions has been a fascinating yet challenging problem. Despite its difficulty, great progress has been made in the past a few years. One class of methods use statistical methods (e.g. PCA) to find a low dimensional subspace to approximate the space of all possible face appearance under different illumination [Cascia et al., 2000, Georghiades et al., 1998, Georghiades et al., 1999, Hallinan, 1994, Riklin-Raviv and Shashua, 1999]. The PCA-based subspace can be used in (1) analysis, such as face tracking [Cascia et al., 2000] and face recognition [Georghiades et al., 1998, Riklin-Raviv and Shashua, 1999] when illumination changes; and (2) synthesize face appearance in different lighting [Georghiades et al., 1999, Riklin-Raviv and Shashua, 1999, Stoschek, 2000]. Recently, Ramamoorthi and Hanrahan [Ramam.. hi and Hanrahan, 2001a] used an analytic expression in terms of spherical harmonic coefficients of the lighting to approximate irradiance and they discovered that only 9 coefficients are needed for the appearance of Lambertian objects. Basri and Jacobs [Basri and Jacobs, 2001] obtained similar theoretical results. Assuming faces are Lambertian, they applied the spherical harmonic basis image in face recognition under variable lighting. Ramamoorthi [Ramamoorthi, 2002] presented an analytic PCA construction of the face appearance under all possible lighting. The results show that the whole space can be well approximated by a subspace spanned by the first five principal components.

To synthesize photo-realistic images of human faces under arbitrary lighting, another class of method is the inverse rendering [Marschner and Greenberg, 1997, Debevec, 1998, Yu et al., 1999, Debevec et al., 2000]. By capturing lighting environment and recovering surface reflectance properties, one can generate photo-realistic rendering of objects including human faces under new lighting conditions. To accurately measure face surface reflectance properties, however, special apparatuses such as "light stage" [Debevec et al., 2000] are usually need to be built.

In this book, we present an efficient method to approximate illumination model from a single face image. Then the illumination model is used for face relighting, that is, rendering faces in various lighting conditions. This method has the advantage that it does not require the separation of illumination from face reflectance, and it is simple to implement and runs at interactive speed.

- Illumination modeling for face recognition

Because illumination affects face appearance significantly, illumination modeling is important for face recognition under varying lighting.

In recent years, there have been works in face recognition community addressing face image variation due to illumination changes [Zhao et al., 2000, Chellappa et al., 1995]. Georghiades et al. [Georghiades et al., 2001] present a new method using the illumination cone. Sim and Kanade [Sim and Kanade, 2001] propose a model and exemplar based approach for recognition. Nonetheless, both [Georghiades et al., 2001] and [Sim and Kanade, 2001] need to reconstruct 3D face information for each subject in the training set. Then they synthesize face images in various lighting to train their face recognizer. Blanz et al. [Blanz et al., 2002] recover the shape and texture parameters of a 3D Morphable Model in an analysis-by-synthesis fashion. These parameters are then used for face recognition. This method needs to compute a statistical texture and shape model from a 3D face database. The illumination effects are modeled by Phong model [Foley and Dam, 1984]. When fitting the 3D morphable face model to an input face image, the illumination parameters are estimated along with texture and shape parameters. However, because there are many parameters to estimate and optimization is non-linear, the fitting is computational expensive and need good initialization.

In general, appearance-based methods such as Eigenfaces [Turk and Pentland, 1991] and AAM [Cootes et al., 1998] need a number of training images for each subject, in order to deal with illumination variability. Previous research suggests that illumination variability in face images is low-dimensional e.g. [Adini et al., 1997, Basri and Jacobs, 2001, Belhumeur and Kriegman, 1998, Ramamoorthi, 2002, Epstein et al., 1995, Hallinan, 1994]. Using spherical harmonics presentation of Lambertian reflection, Basri et al. [Basri and Jacobs, 2001] and Ramamoorthi [Ramamoorthi, 2002] have obtained theoretical derivation of the low dimensional space. Furthermore, a simple scheme for face recognition with excellent results is presented in [Basri and Jacobs, 2001]. However, to use this recognition scheme, the basis images spanning the illumination space for each face are required. These images can be rendered from a 3D scan of the face or can be estimated by applying PCA to a number of images of the same subject under different illuminations [Ramamoorthi, 2002]. An effective approximation of this basis by 9 single light source images of a face is reported in [Lee et al., 2001]. These methods need a number of images and/or 3D scan data of the subjects in the database. Therefore it would requires specialized equipment and procedures for the capture of the training set, thus limiting their applicability. Zhao and Chellappa [Zhao and R.Chellappa, 2000] use symmetric shape-from-shading. But it suffers from the drawbacks of shape-from-shading, such as the assumption of point lighting sources. Zhang and Samaras [Zhang and Samaras, 2003] propose to recover the 9 spherical harmonic basis images from the input image. Nevertheless, the method in [Zhang and Samaras, 2003] needs a 3D database as in [Blanz et al., 2002] to estimate a statistical model of the spherical harmonic basis images.

In our framework, we show that our face relighting technique can be used to normalize the illumination effects in face images. The advantage of the method is that it does not require extra information as in previous methods to model the illumination effects. In our experiment, we demonstrate that this pre-processing step helps reduce error rates in face recognition under varying lighting environments.

1.3.2   Person dependency

Facial appearance variations are highly person-dependent, because the different people have different facial surface properties and different styles of motion. To deal with the variations across different people, one approach is to collect training data from a variety of people. Nonetheless, the amount of data needed to achieve good results could be huge.

For a Lambertian object, the ratio image [Liu et al., 2001a] of its two aligned images removes its surface albedo dependency thus allowing illumination terms (geometry and lighting) to be captured and transferred. Therefore, the subtle appearance changes due to detailed facial motion can be captured independent of the face albedo. Then, the appearance changes can be mapped to people with different albedos.

1.3.3   Online appearance model

The *Expectation-Maximization* (EM) technique [Dempster et al., 1977] is a framework for optimization with partial information. It is widely applied for computing maximum likelihood estimates for parameters in incomplete data models. By alternating between an expectation step (E-step), which finds expected completions of data given the current parameterization, and a maximization step (M-step), which re-estimates parameters on the basis of completed data, the EM algorithm gradually improves the likelihood for the observed data until convergence at a local maximum.

Using the EM framework, Jepson et al. [Jepson et al., 2001] propose an online appearance model, which is updated at every frame by the EM algorithm for adapting to newly observed facial appearance variations. However, only current stable mode of facial appearance is modeled and the non-rigid facial motions are not interpreted by the model.

An analogy of the the appearance model adaption problem in speech recognition domain is speaker adaptation. A good survey can be found in [Woodland, 1999]. One of the most popular schemes is to adjust model parameters such that the likelihood or posterior probability of new adaptation data is maximized. The EM algorithm can usually be used for this maximization process, treating the parameters to be adjusted as "missing" parameters of the model. One type of approach, called *Maximum Likelihood Linear Regression* (MLLR) [Gales and Woodland, 1996], is to linearly transform the parameters of a speaker-independent model such that the likelihood of the adaptation data of a particular person is maximized. MLLR has the advantage that the same linear transformation can be used to update all parameters to be adjusted, even if the number is large. If relatively few parameters to be adjusted, MLLR will be robust and unsupervised adaptation can be used. In practice, research has shown that it is effective to adjust the mean and covariance of the acoustic GMM model using MLLR.

2. Flexible Appearance Model

In this section, we present a flexible appearance model with reduced dependency on illuminations and individuals. We develop an efficient method to model illumination effects from a single face image [Wen et al., 2003]. The illumination model can be used to reduce illumination dependency of the appearance model in both analysis and synthesis. The flexible appearance model also utilize ratio-image technique to reduce person dependency in a principled way [Wen et al., 2003, Wen and Huang, 2003]. We discuss the two components in the Section 2.1 and 2.2. Analysis and synthesis using this flexible model will be presented in Chapter 7 and 8, respectively.

2.1 Reduce illumination dependency based on illumination modeling

2.1.1 Radiance environment map (REM)

Environment map [Greene, 1986, Miller and Hoffman, 1984] is a technique in computer graphics for capturing environment illuminations from all directions using a sphere. The captured lighting environment can be used together with surface reflectance properties (i.e. "Bidirectional Reflectance Distribution Function" (BRDF)) to generate photo-realistic rendering of objects. For applications dealing with images, such as image/video analysis and image-based rendering, it is difficult to recover accurate surface reflectance properties from images. Another issue is that it could be time consuming to integrate illumination and complex surface reflectance properties at rendering time.

In these scenarios, environment maps that pre-integrate with BRDF can be useful. Radiance environment map is proposed by Greene [Greene, 1986] and Cabral et al. [Cabral et al., 1999] for real-time rendering of objects rotating in lighting environment. Given any sphere with constant "Bidirectional Reflectance Distribution Function" (BRDF), its radiance environment map records its reflected radiance for each point on the sphere. Then, for any surface with the same reflectance material as that of the sphere, its reflected radiance at any point can be found from the radiance environment map by simply looking up the normal. This method is very fast and produces photo-realistic results.

One limitation of this method is that one needs to generate a radiance environment map for each different material. For some objects where every point's material may be different, it would be difficult to apply this method. To overcome this limitation, we observe that, for diffuse objects, the ratio image technique [Riklin-Raviv and Shashua, 1999, Liu et al., 2001a] can be used to remove the material dependency of the radiance environment map, thus making it possible to relight surfaces which have variable reflectance properties. Details of the ratio-image technique will be described in Section 2.2.

Given a diffuse sphere of constant reflectance coefficient ρ, let $\mathcal{L}$ denote the distant lighting distribution. The irradiance on the sphere is then a function of normal $\vec{n}$, given by an integral over the upper hemisphere $\Omega(\vec{n})$ at $\vec{n}$.

$$E(\vec{n}) = \int_{\Omega(\vec{n})} \mathcal{L}(\omega)(\vec{n} \cdot \omega) d\omega \qquad (6.1)$$

The intensity of the sphere is

$$I_{sphere}(\vec{n}) = \rho E(\vec{n}) \qquad (6.2)$$

$I_{sphere}(\vec{n})$ is the radiance environment map. Notice that radiance environment map depends on both the lighting and the reflectance coefficient ρ. The intensity of the sphere $I_{sphere}(\vec{n})$ is usually warped to a reference plane to extract 2D image map $I_{sphere}(u, v)$, where (u, v) is the coordinate system of the 2D reference plane.

We can derive similar formulas for face appearance if we assume faces are Lambertian, and ignore cast shadows which is a common assumption for environment map based techniques. Let $\vec{n}(u, v)$, $\rho(u, v)$ denote the normal and albedo of a face surface point at texture plane (u, v). Suppose the face is in the same lighting environment as $I_{sphere}(\vec{n})$. The irradiance on the face is same as $E(\vec{n})$, which can be re-written using coordinate system (u, v) as:

$$E(u, v) = \int_{\Omega(\vec{n}(u,v))} L(\omega)(\vec{n}(u, v) \cdot \omega) d\omega \qquad (6.3)$$

The intensity of the neutral face point p at (u, v) is

$$I(u, v) = \rho(u, v) E(u, v) \qquad (6.4)$$

We can observe that for sphere and face points with the same normal, the pixels intensity can be computed with the same lighting $E(u, v)$. The only difference is the different albedos for the two surfaces, which we can handle using the ratio-image technique described in Section 2.2.

2.1.2 Approximating a radiance environment map using spherical harmonics

A radiance environment map can be captured by taking photographs of a sphere painted with a constant diffuse material. It usually requires multiple views and they need to be stitched together. However, spherical harmonics technique [Ramamoorthi and Hanrahan, 2001a] provides a way to approximate a radiance environment map from one or more images of a sphere or other types of surfaces.

Using the notation of [Ramamoorthi and Hanrahan, 2001a], the irradiance can be represented as a linear combination of spherical harmonic basis functions:

$$E(\vec{n}) = \sum_{l \geq 0, -l \leq m \leq l} \hat{A}_l \, L_{lm} \, Y_{lm}(\vec{n}) \tag{6.5}$$

Ramamoorthi and Hanrahan [Ramamoorthi and Hanrahan, 2001a] showed that for diffuse reflectance, only 9 coefficients are needed to approximate the irradiance function. Therefore, given an image of a diffuse surface with constant albedo ρ, its reflected radiance at a point with normal $\vec{n}$ can be approximated as

$$\rho E(\vec{n}) \approx \sum_{l \leq 2, -l \leq m \leq l} \rho \, \hat{A}_l \, L_{lm} \, Y_{lm}(\vec{n}) \tag{6.6}$$

If we treat $\rho \, \hat{A}_l \, L_{lm}$ as a single variable for each l and m, we can solve for these 9 variables using a least square procedure, thus obtaining the full radiance environment map. This approximation gives a very compact representation of the radiance environment map, using only 9 coefficients per color channel.

An important extension is the type of surface whose albedo, though not constant, does not have low-frequency components (except the constant component). To justify this, we define a function $\rho(\vec{n})$ such that $\rho(\vec{n})$ equals to the average albedo of surface points whose normal is $\vec{n}$. We expand $\rho(\vec{n})$ using spherical harmonics as:

$$\rho(\vec{n}) = \rho_{00} + \Psi(\vec{n}) \tag{6.7}$$

where ρ_{00} is the constant component and $\Psi(\vec{n})$ contains other higher order components. Together with equation (6.6), we have

$$\begin{aligned} \rho(\vec{n})E(\vec{n}) \approx \rho_{00} & \sum_{l \leq 2, -l \leq m \leq l} \hat{A}_l \, L_{lm} \, Y_{lm}(\vec{n}) \\ + \Psi(\vec{n}) & \sum_{l \leq 2, -l \leq m \leq l} \hat{A}_l \, L_{lm} \, Y_{lm}(\vec{n}) \end{aligned} \tag{6.8}$$

If $\Psi(\vec{n})$ does not have first four order ($l = 1, 2, 3, 4$) components, the second term of the righthand side in equation (6.7) contains components with orders equal to or higher than 3 (see Appendix A for the explanation). Therefore, if we define $SpharmonicProj(I)$ to the be function which projects the face image I into the 9 dimensional spherical harmonic space, we have

$$\begin{aligned} SpharmonicProj(I) &= SpharmonicProj(\rho(\vec{n})E(\vec{n})) \\ &= \rho_{00} \sum_{l \leq 2, -l \leq m \leq l} \hat{A}_l \, L_{lm} \, Y_{lm}(\vec{n}) \end{aligned} \tag{6.9}$$

Therefore, the 9 coefficients of order $l \leq 2$ estimated from $\rho(\vec{n})E(\vec{n})$ with a linear least square procedure are $\rho_{00} \, \hat{A}_l \, L_{lm}$, where $(l \leq 2, -l \leq m \leq l)$. Hence,

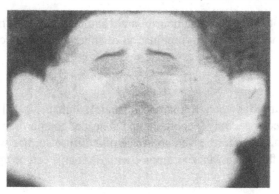

Figure 6.1. A face albedo map.

we obtain the radiance environment map with reflectance coefficient equal to the average albedo of the surface. This observation agrees with [Ramamoorthi and Hanrahan, 2001b] and perception literature (such as Land's retinex theory [Land and McCann, 1971]), where on Lambertian surface high-frequency variation is due to texture, and low-frequency variation probably associated with illumination.

We believe that human face skins are approximately this type of surfaces. The skin color of a person's face has dominant constant component, but there are some fine details corresponding to high frequency components in frequency domain. Therefore the first four order components must be very small. To verify this, we used *SpharmonicKit* [SphericalHarmonic, 2002] to compute the spherical harmonic coefficients for the function $\rho(\vec{n})$ of the albedo map shown in Figure 6.1 which was obtained by Marschner et al. [Marschner et al., 2000]. There are normals that are not sampled by the albedo map, where we assigned $\rho(\vec{n})$ the mean of existing samples. We find that the coefficients of order $1, 2, 3, 4$ components are less than 6% of the constant coefficient.

2.1.3   Approximating a radiance environment map from a single image

Given a single photograph of a person's face, it is possible to compute its 3D geometry [Blanz and Vetter, 1999, Zhang et al., 2001]. Alternatively, we choose to use a generic geometric model (see Figure 8.2(a)) because human faces have similar shapes, and the artifacts due to geometric inaccuracy are not very strong since we only consider diffuse reflections.

Given a photograph and a generic 3D face geometry, we first align the face image with the generic face model. Details of the 2D-3D alignment is discussed in the implementation Section 1.3 of Chapter 8. After the photograph is aligned with the 3D geometry, we know the normal of each face pixel and thus can compute the $Y_{lm}(\vec{n})$ term in equation 6.8. Next, we can solve for the lighting coefficients in equation 6.8 and obtain the approximated radiance environment map.

Note that it is an under-constrained problem to determine all the 9 coefficients from a single frontal image of a face according to [Ramamoorthi, 2002]. To produce plausible illumination approximation results without conflicting with the information provided by the frontal image, we make assumptions about lighting in the back to constrain the problem. One of the assumptions that we make is to assume a symmetric lighting environment, that is, the back has the same lighting distribution as the front. This assumption is equivalent to assuming $L_{lm} = 0$ for $(l, m) = (1, 0), (2, -1), (2, 1)$ in equation (6.6). The rest of the coefficients can then be solved uniquely according to [Ramamoorthi, 2002]. One nice property about this assumption is that it generates the correct lighting results for the front, and it generates plausible results for the back if faces rotate in the lighting environment. For applications which deal with only frontal lighting, the symmetric assumption produces correct results. If we want to synthesize face appearance after the face is rotated in the lighting environment, we need to make the assumption based on the scene. For example, in the cases where the lights mainly come from the two sides of the face, we use symmetric assumptions. In the cases where the lights mainly come from the front, we assume the back is dark.

2.2 Reduce person dependency based on ratio-image technique

2.2.1 Ratio image

In Section 2.1.1, we have derived the formula (equation 6.4) for the intensity of the neutral face point p at (u, v). After the face surface is deformed, the intensity of p is

$$I'(u, v) = \rho(u, v)E'(u, v) \tag{6.10}$$

We denote

$$\Re(u, v) = \frac{I'(u, v)}{I(u, v)} = \frac{E'(u, v)}{E(u, v)} \tag{6.11}$$

It can be observed that $\Re(u, v)$, called the ratio image, is independent of surface reflectance property $\rho(u, v)$ [Liu et al., 2001a]. Therefore, $\Re(u, v)$ can be used to as a facial motion representation independent of face albedos.

2.2.2 Transfer motion details using ratio image

The albedo-independency of ratio image give a novel representation of facial motion field which is less person dependent than the original image. Liu et al. [Liu et al., 2001a] use this property to map facial expressions from one person to another and achieve photo-realistic results.

Given two aligned images of person A's face I_A and I'_A, suppose I_A is the neutral face image and I'_A is the image of the deformed face. Based on equation 6.11, we have

$$\Re_A(u, v) = \frac{I'_A(u, v)}{I_A(u, v)} = \frac{E'_A(u, v)}{E_A(u, v)} \tag{6.12}$$

For a different person B, if we know its neutral face image I_B, we can compute the deformed face image of B where B has the same motion as A. Similarly, we can compute the ratio image for B as

$$\Re_B(u, v) = \frac{I'_B(u, v)}{I_B(u, v)} = \frac{E'_B(u, v)}{E_B(u, v)} \tag{6.13}$$

We assume the images of A and B are aligned, that is, for every point on A, there is a corresponding point on B which has the same semantics (eye corners, mouth corners, etc). This alignment can be done using the techniques described in Section 2.1.3. Since human faces have approximately the same geometrical shapes, their surface normals at corresponding points are roughly the same, that is, $\vec{n}_A(u, v) \approx \vec{n}_B(u, v)$. We also assume that the deformation of the two faces are roughly the same. Then we have $\vec{n}'_A(u, v) \approx \vec{n}'_B(u, v)$. Based on equation 6.3, we can derive $E_A(u, v) \approx E_B(u, v)$ and $E'_A(u, v) \approx E'_B(u, v)$. That leads to

$$\Re_A(u, v) \approx \Re_B(u, v) \tag{6.14}$$

From equations 6.12, 6.13 and 6.14, we can compute the unknown image I'_B as

$$I'_B \approx \Re_A(u, v) I_B \tag{6.15}$$

Here the multiplication means pixel-by-pixel multiplication of the two images.

Besides computing novel face image I'_B for synthesis, ratio image can also be used to design less person dependent appearance features for motion analysis. This aspect will be discussed in more details in Chapter 7.

2.2.3   Transfer illumination using ratio image

The albedo-independency of ratio image also enables illumination effects transfer across different surfaces. Wen et al. [Wen et al., 2003] use this property for face relighting from a single face image.

Following the derivation in Section 2.2.2, if the difference between I_A and I'_A is illumination effects instead of non-rigid motion, we can obtain the same equation 6.15 for computing novel face appearance I'_B in the lighting environment of I'_A. More generally, A could be other objects such as the sphere of radiance environment map. Then we can use the REM illumination model together with equation 6.15 for modifying illumination effects in face images.

3. Summary

In this chapter, we have reviewed related works on using appearance models for face analysis and synthesis. Then, we introduce our flexible appearance model, which contains two components for reducing dependencies on illuminations and individuals. We will present our facial motion analysis using the flexible appearance model in Chapter 7. Flexible appearance model based synthesis will be discussed in Chapter 8.

Chapter 7

FACIAL MOTION ANALYSIS USING FLEXIBLE APPEARANCE MODEL

In this chapter, we discuss the face motion analysis using flexible appearance model described in Chapter 6. Our goal is to utilize appearance cues to improve the detection and classification of subtle motions which exhibit similar geometric features. For this purpose, we design novel appearance features for the analysis of these detailed motions. Compared with most existing appearance features, our appearance features are less illumination dependent and less person dependent. In our facial expression classification experiment, we show that this appearance features improve the classification performance under variations in lighting, 3D poses and person.

In Section 1, we first describe the proposed novel appearance features and explain how the dependencies on illumination and person are reduced. Then we describe an online appearance model adaptation scheme to further improve the performance in changing conditions. Next, in Section 2, experimental results on facial expression recognition are presented to demonstrate the efficacy of the novel appearance features.

1.   Model-based 3D Face Motion Analysis Using Both Geometry and Appearance

Given a face video, we can employ both geometric and appearance features to analyze the facial motions. The system diagram for the hybrid motion analysis is illustrated in figure 7.1. First, we use a geometric-based method described in Chapter 4 to estimate 3D geometric deformation. The geometric deformation features are extracted as the coefficients of MUs. Figure 7.2(b) shows a snapshot of the geometric tracking system, where a yellow mesh is used to visualize the geometric motions of the face. The input video frame is shown in Figure 7.2(a).

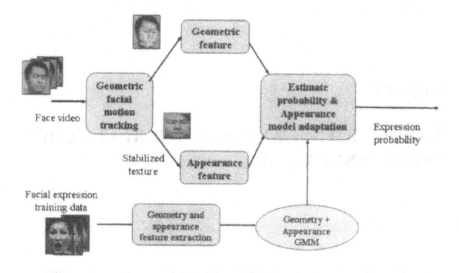

Figure 7.1.   Hybrid 3D face motion analysis system.

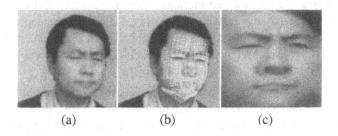

(a)   (b)   (c)

Figure 7.2.   (a): The input video frame. (b): The snapshot of the geometric tracking system. (c): The extracted texture map

The geometric deformation parameters determine the registration of each image frame to the face texture map. Thus we can derive a face texture map $I(u, v)$ from each image frame, which are independent of geometric motion. Here, (u, v) is the coordinate system of the texture map. Figure 7.2(c) shows the extracted texture map. From the texture maps, we extract appearance-based features described in Section 1.1. These features are designed for subtle details of facial expression and independent of people's face surface albeo. We then use the texture (appearance) features, together with shape (geometric) features, to analyze face appearance variations based on semantically meaningful exemplars.

To extend a trained appearance-based exemplar model to new conditions, an online EM-based algorithm is used to update the appearance model of these exemplars progressively.

1.1 Feature extraction

We assume faces are Lambertian. Let $I(u, v)$, $I'(u, v)$ denote the neutral face texture and deformed face texture, respectively. We denote

$$\Re(u, v) = \frac{I'(u, v)}{I(u, v)} \tag{7.1}$$

As pointed out by Section 2.2.1 of Chapter 6, the ratio image $\Re(u, v)$ is independent of surface reflectance property $\rho(u, v)$ [Liu et al., 2001a]. Therefore, $\Re(u, v)$ can be used to characterize facial motions of faces with different albedos.

To use $\Re(u, v)$ in face tracking, more compact features need to be extracted from the high dimensional ratio image. Because low frequency variation of facial motion could be captured by geometric-based methods, we extract features from $\Re(u, v)$ in frequency domain and use the high frequency components as the features for motions not explained by geometric features. Second, past studies on facial motions [Zhang et al., 1998, Tian et al., 2002] have shown that there are certain facial areas where high frequency appearance changes are more likely to occur and thus suitable for texture feature extraction. We apply this domain knowledge in our feature extraction. However, because of noise in tracking and individual variation, it is difficult to locate these locations automatically with enough precision. Therefore, we extract the texture-based features in facial regions instead of points, and then use the weighted average as the final feature. Eleven regions are defined on the geometric-motion-free texture map. These eleven regions are highlighted on the texture map in Fig. 7.3. Note that these regions can be considered constant in the automatically extracted texture map, where the facial feature points are aligned by geometric tracking.

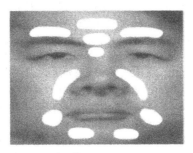

Figure 7.3. Selected facial regions for feature extraction.

Gabor wavelets are used to extract the appearance changes as a set of multi-scale and multi-orientation coefficients. In our implementation, we use two spatial frequency scales with wavelength of 5 and 8 pixels, and 6 orientations at each scale. Thus for each point, we have $2 \times 6 = 12$ Gabor wavelets coefficients. We choose to compute the Gabor wavelets coefficients of the logarithm of $\Re(u, v)$, denoted by $Z(u, v)$. Based on equation (7.1) and the linearity property of Gabor transform, we have

$$
\begin{aligned}
Z(u, v) &= G(\log(\Re(u, v))) \\
&= G(\log(I'(u, v))) - G(\log(I(u, v)))
\end{aligned}
\tag{7.2}
$$

where function G denotes a Gabor transform as in [Tian et al., 2002, Zhang et al., 1998]. We impose a positive lower bound on pixel values in texture I' and I to avoid singular situations. In our approach, only the magnitudes of Gabor transform results are used because the phases are very sensitive to noise in positions. Then we note that if $Z(u, v) < 0$, it means the neutral face texture I contains more high frequency components than the deformed face texture I'. It could be caused by any of the following reasons: (1) the misalignment of I' and I; (2) high gradient of $\log(I)$ due to low intensities of I; (3) flattening of wrinkles and creases on neutral face during motion. Scenarios (1) and (2) should be considered as noise, and (3) rarely happens in common human facial motions. Thus we discard negative values of $Z(u, v)$.

In practice, we need to account for the foreshortening effect of the texture projection. For a 3D face surface patch, the larger its visible area in input image, the higher confidence we should have on the extracted features of the corresponding texture patch. To this end, we construct a confidence map $\kappa(u, v)$ following [Cascia et al., 2000], which is based on the ratio of each 3D surface patch's projected area in the texture plane and its area in the input image. For each facial motion region q ($q = 1...11$), we compute a confidence coefficient c_q as the average of the $\kappa(u, v)$ in this region. The resulting confidence coefficients are used to weight the features in tracking described in Section 1.3.

$\Re(u, v)$ contains noise due to misalignment of I' and I. To reduce the influences of noise on the appearance feature, we construct another weight map $w(u, v)$, which tries to give large weight for features in deformed area and small weight for features in un-deformed area. We define $w(u, v) = 1 - corr(u, v)$ in similar spirit as [Liu et al., 2001a], where $corr(u, v)$ is the normalized cross-correlation coefficient between two patches centered at (u, v) from $G(\log(I'))$ and $G(\log(I))$. The idea is that high frequency components of $\log(I')$ and $\log(I)$ should be close for un-deformed area, since I' and I are roughly aligned by geometric-feature-based tracking. We use $w(u, v)$ to compute the weighted average of Gabor wavelets coefficients in the 11 selected regions. For each region, an appearance feature vector of 12-dimension is computed.

1.2 Influences of lighting

Under the assumptions of Lambertian faces, distant illumination and ignoring cast shadows, the proposed appearance features are not sensitive to changes of lighting conditions. According to [Basri and Jacobs, 2001, Ramamoorthi and Hanrahan, 2001b], the irradiance can be represented by a linear combination of spherical harmonic basis function. For Lambertian surfaces, only the first 2 orders of the basis functions (9 basis) are needed to approximate the irradiance, that is

$$E(u,v) \approx \sum_{l \leq 2, -l \leq m \leq l} \hat{A}_l L_{lm} Y_{lm}(\vec{n}(u,v)) \qquad (7.3)$$

where $\hat{A}_l$ is a constant, L_{lm} is a coefficient decided by lighting, and Y_{lm} is the spherical harmonic basis function. Assuming that neutral face and the deformed face are in the same lighting condition, we have

$$
\begin{aligned}
\Re(u,v) &= \frac{E'(u,v)}{E(u,v)} \\
&\approx \frac{\sum_{l \leq 2, -l \leq m \leq l} \hat{A}_l L_{lm} Y_{lm}(\vec{n'}(u,v))}{\sum_{l \leq 2, -l \leq m \leq l} \hat{A}_l L_{lm} Y_{lm}(\vec{n}(u,v))}
\end{aligned} \qquad (7.4)
$$

The high frequency facial motion $d_H(u,v)$ can produce high frequency differences between $\vec{n'}(u,v)$ and $\vec{n}(u,v)$, and therefore between $Y_{lm}(\vec{n'}(u,v))$ and $Y_{lm}(\vec{n}(u,v))$. The irradiance $E'(u,v)$ will contain a linear combination of these high frequency differences weighted by the lighting coefficients. In other words, high frequency changes in $\Re(u,v)$ are due to facial deformation details, while lighting will only modulate them in low frequency. If the neutral face and the deformed face are in different lighting conditions, the neutral face texture can be relit to the lighting of the deformed face using face relighting technique in [Wen et al., 2003]. According to [Wen et al., 2003], the relighting is a low-frequency filtering processing so that the above arguments are still true.

1.3 Exemplar-based texture analysis

The appearance model are designed to model facial motion details that are not captured by low dimensional geometric models. These motion details exhibit much larger variation than geometric motions across different individuals and lighting conditions. Thus a good low-dimensional subspace approximation of motion details variation may be difficult. Nevertheless, facial motions exhibit common semantic exemplars such as typical expressions and visemes, which makes it meaningful to use exemplar-based approach such as [Toyama and Blake, 2002]. In exemplar-based approach, an observation is interpreted using the probability of the observation being each exemplar.

To explain the face appearance variation, we choose exemplars set $\Xi = \{x_k, k = 1, ..., K\}$, which are semantically meaningful such as face expressions or visemes. A texture image is interpreted as a state variable X of the exemplars. Unlike [Toyama and Blake, 2002], these exemplars incur both shape and texture changes. Let Y_S and Y_T denote the shape and texture features respectively. The observation is $Y = \{Y_S, Y_T\}$. We assume Y_S and Y_T are conditionally independent given X. The observation likelihood is

$$p(Y|X) = p(Y_S, Y_T|X) = p(Y_S|X)\,p(Y_T|X) \qquad (7.5)$$

In addition, we assume the texture features in different facial motion regions are independent given X. Their log likelihoods are weighted by confidence coefficients c_q to account for foreshortening effect. That is

$$\log p(Y_T|X) = \sum_{q=1}^{Q} c_q \, \log p(Y_{T_q}|X) \qquad (7.6)$$

where Q is the number of facial motion regions ($Q = 11$). $p(Y_S|X)$ and $p(Y_{T_q}|X)$ are modelled using Gaussian Mixture Model (GMM), assuming diagonal covariance matrices. The feature vectors are normalized by their magnitudes. If the neutral face is chosen as an exemplar, we assign the likelihood using a neutral face classifier such as [Tian and Bolle, 2001].

Based on the observation likelihoods in equation (7.5) and a dynamics model (e.g. the HMM-based model described in [Toyama and Blake, 2002]), $p_t(X_t) \equiv p_t(X_t|Y_1, ..., Y_t)$ can be computed using equation (7.7) according to [Rabiner, 1989]

$$p_t(X_t) = \sum_{X_{t-1}=1}^{K} p(Y_t|X_t)\,p(X_t|X_{t-1})\,p_{t-1}(X_{t-1}) \qquad (7.7)$$

In our experiment, we assume uniform conditional density $p(X_t|X_{t-1})$ for the dynamics model. Assuming uniform priors, we have $p_t(X_t) \propto p(Y_{S_t}, Y_{T_t}|X_t)$. The exemplar tracking result can be displayed as $\hat{X}_t = \arg\max p_t(X_t)$.

1.4   Online EM-based adaptation

A trained model for facial motion exemplars may work poorly if it can not adapt to lighting changes, or differences in a new individual's exemplars. Fast adaptation algorithm is needed to avoid re-training the model from scratch. Furthermore, it is tedious to collect and label new training data for each new condition. Therefore, we propose to progressively update the model during tracking in an unsupervised way. Because the geometric features are less person-dependent and less sensitive to lighting changes, we assume the geometric component of the initial exemplar model can help to "confidently" track some new data samples. Then the Expectation-Maximization (EM) framework [Dempster et al., 1977] can be applied to update the model parameters. At time t, the E-step provides exemplar ownership probabilities defined as

$$o_{k,t}(Y_t) = \frac{p(Y_t|X_t = k)}{\sum_{k=1}^{K} p(Y_t|X_t = k)} \tag{7.8}$$

where k is the index of the exemplars. In the M-step, the model is adapted by computing new maximum likelihood estimates of its parameters. Note that we only adapt the texture part of the model because shape features are less person-dependent and not sensitive to changes of lighting.

The idea of Maximum Likelihood Linear Regression (MLLR) can be generalized to this adaptation problem, where we estimate a linear transformation of the GMM mean vectors to maximize the likelihood of new observations. However, conventional MLLR is not an online method which requires multiple data samples for maximum likelihood optimization. In the M-step of our online EM algorithm, only one data sample is available at a time. Thus we constrain the transformation of the GMM mean vectors to be translation only. The M-step of our algorithm is then to estimate $\Delta\mu_{q,k,t}$, which denotes the translation of the GMM mean vectors from initial model, for the qth facial motion region, the kth exemplar at time t. To weight the current data sample appropriately against history, we consider the data samples under an exponential envelope located at the current time as in [Jepson et al., 2001], $F_t(j) = \alpha e^{-(t-j)/\tau}$, for $j \leq t$. Here, $\alpha = 1 - e^{-1/\tau}$.

For the GMM model of certain (q, k, t) value, suppose the GMM has M components denoted by $\{N(\mu_1, \Sigma_1), ..., N(\mu_M, \Sigma_M)\}$. Here the q, k, t subscripts are dropped for simplicity. Given an adaptation data sample $Y = \{Y_S, Y_T\}$, the ML estimate of the translation $\Delta\mu$ can be computed by solving equation (7.9) according to [Gales and Woodland, 1996]:

$$\sum_{m=1}^{M} \gamma_m \Sigma_m^{-1} Y_T \mu_m^T = \sum_{m=1}^{M} \gamma_m \Sigma_m^{-1} (\mu_m + \Delta\mu) \mu_m^T \tag{7.9}$$

where γ_m is GMM component occupancy probability defined as the probability that Y_T draws from the mth component of the GMM given Y_T draws from this GMM. Y_T is the texture feature of the current adaptation data. A closed-form solution for equation (7.9) is feasible when Σ_m is diagonal. The ith element of $\Delta\mu$ can be computed as

$$\Delta\mu_i = \frac{\sum_{m=1}^{M} \gamma_m \sigma_{m,i} Y_{T_i} - \sum_{m=1}^{M} \gamma_m \sigma_{m,i} \mu_{m,i}}{\sum_{m=1}^{M} \gamma_m \sigma_{m,i}} \tag{7.10}$$

where $\sigma_{m,i}$ is the ith diagonal element of Σ_m^{-1}, and Y_{T_i} is the ith element of Y_T.

The probability weighted average of the translation vector up to time t, for the kth exemplar of a certain facial motion region is then

$$\Delta \bar{\mu}_{k,t} = \frac{1}{\beta_{k,t}} (\sum_{j=-\infty}^{t} F_t(j) o_{k,t}(Y_j) \Delta \mu_{k,j}) \qquad (7.11)$$

where $\beta_{k,t}$ is a normalization factor defined as $\beta_{k,t} = \sum_{j=-\infty}^{t} F_t(j) o_{k,t}(Y_j)$, and $\Delta \mu_{k,j}$ is computed using equation (7.10). Equation (7.11) can be rewritten in a recursive manner as:

$$\Delta \bar{\mu}_{k,t} = \frac{(1-\alpha) \beta_{k,t-1} \Delta \bar{\mu}_{k,t-1} + \alpha\, o_{k,t}(Y_t) \Delta \mu_{k,t}}{\beta_{k,t}} \qquad (7.12)$$

where $\beta_{k,t} = (1-\alpha) \beta_{k,t-1} + \alpha\, o_{k,t}(Y_t)$. Equations (7.10) and (7.12) are applied to updated the translation vectors of each facial motion region.

In an online EM algorithm, the training samples can not be used iteratively for optimization. Thus, errors made by the initial model may cause the adaptation method to be unstable. Note that the chosen exemplars are common semantic symbols which have their intrinsic structure. Therefore, when adapting the exemplar model to a particular person, the translations of the mean vectors should be constrained rather than random. For the exemplars model of a facial motion region at time t, let ξ denote the translation vector constructed by concatenating the translations of all the mean vectors, i.e., $\xi = [\Delta \mu_1^T \ldots \Delta \mu_K^T]^T$, where K is the number of exemplars. In our algorithm, ξ is a 72-dimension vector. We impose the constraint that the vector ξ should lie in certain low dimensional subspaces. To learn such a low dimensional subspace, we first learn a person-independent exemplar model from exemplars of many people. Then a person-dependent exemplar model is learned for each person. We collect a training sample set $\{\xi\}$, consisting of the translation vectors between the mean vectors of person-independent model and person-dependent models. Finally, PCA is applied on the set $\{\xi\}$. Principal orthogonal components which account for major variation in set $\{\xi\}$ are chosen to span a low dimensional subspace. A translation vector can be projected to the learned subspace by

$$a = W^T (\xi - \bar{\xi}) \qquad (7.13)$$

and the new constrained translation vector can be reconstructed as

$$\hat{\xi} = W a + \bar{\xi} \qquad (7.14)$$

where W is the matrix consisting of principal orthogonal components, $\bar{\xi}$ is the mean translation vector of the vectors in $\{\xi\}$.

In summary, the online EM-based adaptation algorithm is as follows:

- E-step: compute exemplar ownership probabilities $o_{k,t}(Y_t)$ based on equations (7.5), (7.6) and (7.8).

- M-step: for the qth facial motion region, estimate the translator vector $\Delta\mu_{q,k,t}$ based on equations (7.10) and (7.12). Then we construct the vector $\xi_{q,t}$ and project it using equation (7.13). Finally, the constrained estimate of $\hat{\xi}_{q,t}$ is given by equation (7.14).

2. Experimental Results

We evaluate the efficacy of the proposed hybrid motion analysis method by using the extracted features in a facial expression classifications task. The public available CMU Cohn-Kanade expression database [Kanade et al., 2000] is used. From the database, we selected 47 subjects who has at least 4 coded expression sequences. Overall the selected database contains 2981 frames. There are 72% female, 28% male, 89% Euro-American, 9% Afro-American, and 2% Asian. Several different lighting conditions are present in the selected database. The image size of all the data is 640 × 480. For the Cohn-Kanade database, Tian and Bolle [Tian and Bolle, 2001] achieved a high neutral face detection rate using geometric features only. That indicates the database does not contain expressions with little geometric motion yet large texture variation. Using geometric feature only on the database, Cohen et al. [Cohen et al., 2003] reported good recognition results for happiness and surprise, but much more confusion among anger, disgust, fear and sadness. In this section, we present our experimental results showing the proposed method improves the performance for these four expressions.

We select seven exemplars including six expressions and *neutral*. The six expressions are anger, disgust, fear, happiness, sadness, and surprise. In our experiments, we first assign *neutral* vs. non-*neutral* probability using a neutral network similar to [Tian and Bolle, 2001], which achieved a recognition rate of 92.8% for *neutral*. For the remaining exemplars, we use 4 components for each GMM model. The tracking results are used to perform facial expression classification as $\hat{X}_t = \arg\max p_t(X_t)$. Although this classifier may not be as good as more sophisticated classifiers such as those in [Bartlett et al., 1999, Cohen et al., 2003, Donato et al., 1999, Zhang et al., 1998], it can be used as a test-bed to measure the relative performances of different features and the proposed adaptation algorithm.

In the first experiment, we compare the classification performances of using geometric feature only and using both geometric and ratio-image-based appearance features. We use 60% data of each person as training data and the rest as test data. Thus it is a person-dependent test. For all experiments we have done, geometric-feature-only method and hybrid-feature method give similar results for "happiness" and "surprise". That means these two expressions have distinct geometric features so that appearance features are not crucial for them. This observation is consistent with [Cohen et al., 2003]. Therefore, in this section we choose to omit the results for "happiness" and "surprise" for conciseness.

The confusion matrix for the geometric-feature-only method is presented in Table 7.1. In Table 7.2, we show the confusion matrix for the method using both appearance and geometric features. Note that we omit the rows of "happiness" and "surprise" for conciseness. The analysis of the confusion between different expressions shows that the proposed appearance features help to significantly reduce the confusion among expressions, especially the four more easily confused expressions: anger, disgust, fear and sadness. For example, the confusion rate between "anger" and "disgust" is reduced more than 10 percent. This improvement demonstrate the effectiveness of the proposed appearance features in handling motion details.

Expressions	Anger	Disgust	Fear	Sadness	Happiness	Surprise
Anger	**74.8%**	13.3%	0%	10.6%	0.7%	0.7%
Disgust	16.3%	**76.5%**	3.1%	4.1%	0%	0%
Fear	0%	0.8%	**65.6%**	5.0%	22.7%	5.9%
Sadness	13.4%	0.6%	2.6%	**77.1%**	0%	6.4%

Table 7.1. Person-dependent confusion matrix using the geometric-feature-only method

Expressions	Anger	Disgust	Fear	Sadness	Happiness	Surprise
Anger	**92.7%**	2.0%	0%	4.6%	0%	0.7%
Disgust	4.1%	**85.7%**	6.1%	3.1%	1.0%	0%
Fear	0%	1.7%	**81.5%**	0%	12.6%	4.2%
Sadness	3.8%	0%	3.2%	**90.5%**	0%	2.5%

Table 7.2. Person-dependent confusion matrix using both geometric and appearance features

In Table 7.3, we show the comparison of the recognition rates for the four easily confused expressions. A more intuitive comparison is illustrated in Figure 7.4.

Expressions	Anger	Disgust	Fear	Sadness
Geo-only	74.8%	76.5%	65.6%	77.1%
Proposed	92.7%	85.7%	81.5%	90.5%

Table 7.3. Comparison of the proposed approach with geometric-only method in person-dependent test.

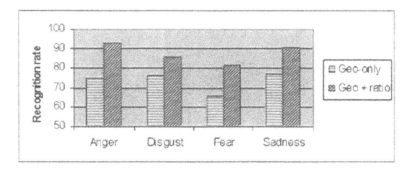

Figure 7.4. Comparison of the proposed approach with geometric-only method in person-dependent test.

In the second experiment, we compare the classification performances of ratio-image based appearance feature and non-ratio-image based appearance feature. The goal of this test is to see whether the proposed appearance feature is less person-dependent. The non-ratio-image based feature does not consider the neutral face texture, and is computed as $G(\log(I'(u, v)))$ instead of using equation (7.1). To show the advantage of ratio-image based feature in the ability to generalize to new people, the test is done in a person-independent way. That is, all data of one person is used as test data and the rest as training data. This test is repeated 47 times, each time leaving a different person out (leave one out cross validation). The person-independent test is more challenging because the variations between subjects are much larger than those within the same subject. To factor out the influence of geometric feature, only the appearance feature is used for recognition in this experiment. The average recognition rates are shown in Table 7.4 and Figure 7.5. We can see that ratio-image based feature outperforms non-ratio-image based feature significantly. For individual subject, we found that the results of the two features are close when the texture does not have much details. Otherwise, ratio-image based feature is much better.

Expressions	Anger	Disgust	Fear	Sadness
ratio	37.0%	59.6%	35.7%	41.8%
non-ratio	24.7%	22.1%	24.4%	15.6%

Table 7.4. Comparison of the proposed appearance feature (ratio) with non-ratio-image based appearance feature (non-ratio) in person-independent recognition test.

The third experiment again uses person-independent setting and leave one out cross validation. For each test, we use 50% of the data of the test person as adaptation data and the rest as test data. Without applying adaptation algorithm,

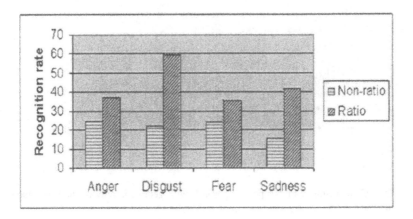

Figure 7.5. Comparison of the proposed appearance feature (ratio) with non-ratio-image based appearance feature (non-ratio) in person-independent recognition test.

we first compare the performances of using geometric feature only and using both geometric and ratio-image-based appearance features. The results are shown in the rows (a) and (b) of Table 7.5. It can be observed that improvement is less significant than that in the first experiment. This is mainly due to the individual variations in facial expressions. Then, We test the performance of the proposed online EM-based adaptation algorithm. Only the models of the four easily confused expressions are adapted. In each test, we apply PCA to the training data. The first 11 principal components are selected which account for about 90% of total variations. The adaptation is online and unsupervised, without using the labels of the adaptation data. We choose $\alpha = 0.1$ for fast adaptation because the amount of the adaptation data is limited. The recognition rates the adaptation are shown in the row (d) of Table 7.5. We can see the adaption algorithm improves the recognition rates. For comparison, we also show in the row (c) the recognition rates of adaptation without the PCA subspace constraints. It can be seen that the unconstrained adaptation is not stable. The performance with unconstrained adaptation could sometimes be worse than performance without adaptation. Figure 7.6 gives a more intuitive comparison of the four methods.

To test the proposed method under large 3D rigid motions and novel lighting conditions, we also collect two video sequences of a subject who is not in the training database. The frame size of the videos is 640 × 480. The first video has 763 frames and contains substantial global face translation and rotation. The second video has 435 frames and is taken under a lighting condition dramatically different from the rest of data. We manually label the image frames using the seven categories as the ground truth. Two snapshots for each sequence are shown in Fig. 7.7 and 7.8. The corresponding recognition results are also

Expressions	Anger	Disgust	Fear	Sadness
a	66.6%	65.3%	60.8%	69.8%
b	70.7%	70.2%	64.6%	72.5%
c	75.3%	59.2%	64.0%	73.1%
d	77.9%	78.1%	67.7%	77.8%

Table 7.5. Comparison of different algorithms in person-independent recognition test. (a): Algorithm uses geometric feature only. (b): Algorithm uses both geometric and ratio-image based appearance feature. (c): Algorithm applies unconstrained adaptation. (d): Algorithm applies constrained adaptation.

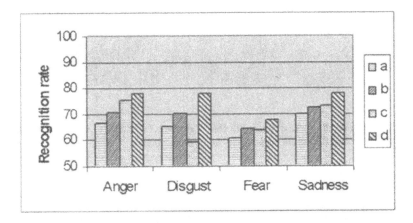

Figure 7.6. Comparison of different algorithms in person-independent recognition test. (a): Algorithm uses geometric feature only. (b): Algorithm uses both geometric and ratio-image based appearance feature. (c): Algorithm applies unconstrained adaptation. (d): Algorithm applies constrained adaptation.

illustrated using one of the training example. We compare the expression recognition rates of the proposed method with geometric-feature-only method. The overall average recognition rate of our method is 71%, while the rate of the geometric-only method is 59%. Part of the tracking results is visualized in the accompanying videos [Wen and Huang, 2004]. In the videos, the upper left of the frame is the input video frame, the upper right is the geometric feature based tracking visualized by a yellow mesh. The exemplar $\hat{X}_t$ is shown on the bottom. We can observe that our method can still track the textu.. .ariations when there are large 3D motions, or under dramatically different lighting conditions.

3. Summary

In this chapter, a hybrid facial motion analysis scheme is presented. In this scheme, we propose a novel appearance feature based on our flexible appearance

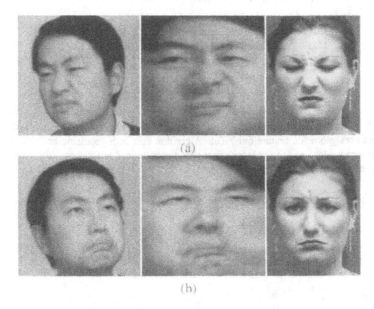

Figure 7.7. The results under different 3D poses. For both (a) and (b): Left: cropped input frame. Middle: extracted texture map. Right: recognized expression.

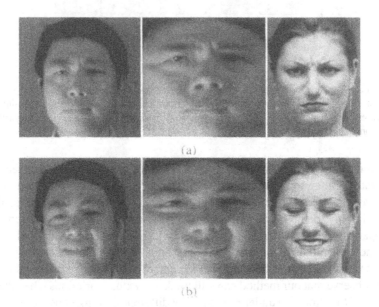

Figure 7.8. The results in a different lighting condition. For both (a) and (b): Left: cropped input frame. Middle: extracted texture map. Right: recognized expression.

model. Compared to most existing appearance features, the novel appearance feature is less illumination dependent and less person dependent. An online appearance model adaptation scheme is also introduced to improve the performance in changing conditions. A facial expression recognition experiment has been conducted to demonstrate the efficacy of the proposed scheme in changing conditions. The recognition performance is improved because of the reduced dependency of the novel appearance feature and the online adaptation scheme.

Chapter 8

FACE APPEARANCE SYNTHESIS USING FLEXIBLE APPEARANCE MODEL

In this chapter, we discuss the face appearance synthesis using flexible appearance model described in Chapter 6. Our goal is to use appearance model in a flexible way to synthesize plausible facial appearance variations caused by lighting and motion. The synthesized appearance can provide visual cues in synthetic face based interactions. For this purpose, the appearance models need to be applicable for different lighting conditions and people. Because we aim at reproducing important visual cues related to facial motion, we neglect less essential phenomena such as specular reflection and assume faces are Lambertian.

In Section 1, we first describe how to synthesize the illumination effects of neutral face appearance in different lighting conditions. Next, we describe works on using the face relighting technique for face recognition under varying lighting conditions 2. In Section 3 the synthesis of facial appearance caused by motion is discussed.

1. Neutral Face Relighting

We present a ratio-image based technique [Wen et al., 2003] to use a radiance environment map to render diffuse objects with different surface reflectance properties. This method has the advantage that it does not require the separation of illumination from reflectance, and it is simple to implement and runs at interactive speed. In order to use this technique for human face relighting, we have developed a technique that uses spherical harmonics to approximate the radiance environment map for any given image of a face. Thus we are able to relight face images when the lighting environment rotates. Another benefit of the radiance environment map is that we can interactively modify lighting by changing the coefficients of the spherical harmonics basis. Finally we can modify the lighting condition of one person's face so that it matches the new lighting condition of a different person's face image assuming the two faces have similar skin albedos.

1.1   Relighting with radiance environment maps

Using the technique described in Section 2.1.3 of Chapter 6, the radiance environment map (REM) based illumination model can be approximated from a single face image. Based on the illumination model, we can then synthesize face image in novel lighting environments in various scenarios, including: (1) face rotating in the same lighting environment; (2) illumination effects transfer from one face to another; and (3) interactively lighting effects editing.

1.1.1   Relighting when rotating in the same lighting condition

When an object is rotated in the same lighting condition, the intensity of the object will change due to incident lighting changes. let $E(\vec{n})$ denote the irradiance defined by equation 6.1. For any given point p on the object, suppose its normal is rotated from $\vec{n_a}$ to $\vec{n_b}$. Assuming the object is diffuse, and let ρ_p denote the reflectance coefficient at p, then the intensities at p before and after rotation are respectively:

$$I_{object}(\vec{n_a}) = \rho_p E(\vec{n_a}) \qquad (8.1)$$

$$I_{object}(\vec{n_b}) = \rho_p E(\vec{n_b}) \qquad (8.2)$$

From equation 8.1 and 8.2 we have

$$\frac{I_{object}(\vec{n_b})}{I_{object}(\vec{n_a})} = \frac{E(\vec{n_b})}{E(\vec{n_a})} \qquad (8.3)$$

From the definition of the radiance environment map (equation 6.2), we have

$$\frac{I_{sphere}(\vec{n_b})}{I_{sphere}(\vec{n_a})} = \frac{E(\vec{n_b})}{E(\vec{n_a})} \qquad (8.4)$$

Comparing equation 8.3 and 8.4, we have

$$\frac{I_{sphere}(\vec{n_b})}{I_{sphere}(\vec{n_a})} = \frac{I_{object}(\vec{n_b})}{I_{object}(\vec{n_a})} \qquad (8.5)$$

What this equation says is that for any point on the object, the ratio between its intensity after rotation and its intensity before rotation is equal to the intensity ratio of two points on the radiance environment map. Therefore given the old intensity $I_{object}(\vec{n_a})$ (before rotation), we can obtain the new intensity $I_{object}(\vec{n_b})$ from the following equation:

$$I_{object}(\vec{n_b}) = \frac{I_{sphere}(\vec{n_b})}{I_{sphere}(\vec{n_a})} \cdot I_{object}(\vec{n_a}) \tag{8.6}$$

Note that the REM I_{sphere} could be approximated from a single input face image.

1.1.2 Comparison with inverse rendering approach

It is interesting to compare our method with the inverse rendering approach. Here we take the face rotating scenario as an example. To use inverse rendering approach, we can capture the illumination environment map, and use spherical harmonics technique [Ramamoorthi and Hanrahan, 2001a] to obtain $E(\vec{n})$: the diffuse components of the irradiance environment map. The reflectance coefficient ρ_p at point p can be resolved from its intensity before rotation and the irradiance, that is,

$$\rho_p = \frac{I_{object}(\vec{n_a})}{E(\vec{n_a})} \tag{8.7}$$

After rotation, its intensity is equal to $\rho_p E(\vec{n_b})$. From equation (8.7) and 8.4,

$$\begin{aligned} \rho_p E(\vec{n_b}) &= I_{object}(\vec{n_a}) \frac{E(\vec{n_b})}{E(\vec{n_a})} \\ &= \frac{I_{sphere}(\vec{n_b})}{I_{sphere}(\vec{n_a})} \cdot I_{object}(\vec{n_a}) \end{aligned}$$

Thus, as expected, we obtain the same formula as equation (8.6).

The difference between our approach and the inverse rendering approach is that our approach only requires a radiance environment map, while the inverse rendering approach requires the illumination environment map (or irradiance environment map). In some cases where only limited amount of data about the lighting environment is available (such as a few photographs of some diffuse objects), it would be difficult to separate illuminations from reflectance properties to obtain illumination environment map. Our technique allows us to do image-based relighting of diffuse objects even from a single image.

1.1.3 Relighting in different lighting conditions

Let $\mathcal{L}$, $\mathcal{L}'$ denote the old and new lighting distributions respectively. Suppose we use the same material to capture the radiance environment maps for both lighting conditions. Let I_{sphere} and I'_{sphere} denote the radiance environment maps of the old and new lighting conditions, respectively. For any point p on the object with normal $\vec{n}$, its old and new intensity values are respectively:

$$I_{object}(\vec{n}) = \rho_p \int_{\Omega(\vec{n})} \mathcal{L}(\omega)(\vec{n} \cdot \omega) d\omega \qquad (8.8)$$

$$I'_{object}(\vec{n}) = \rho_p \int_{\Omega(\vec{n})} \mathcal{L}'(\omega)(\vec{n} \cdot \omega) d\omega \qquad (8.9)$$

Together with equation 6.1 and 6.2, we have a formula of the ratio of the two intensity values

$$\frac{I'_{object}(\vec{n})}{I_{object}(\vec{n})} = \frac{I'_{sphere}(\vec{n})}{I_{sphere}(\vec{n})} \qquad (8.10)$$

Therefore the intensity at p under new lighting condition can be computed as

$$I'_{object}(\vec{n}) = \frac{I'_{sphere}(\vec{n})}{I_{sphere}(\vec{n})} \cdot I_{object}(\vec{n}) \qquad (8.11)$$

1.1.4   Interactive face relighting

In [Ramamoorthi and Hanrahan, 2001a] spherical harmonic basis functions of irradiance environment map were visualized on sphere intuitively, which makes it easy to modify lighting by manually changing the coefficients. Our radiance environment map is the irradiance environment map scaled by constant albedo. We can modify the coefficients in equation (6.6) to interactively create novel radiance environment maps. Then these radiance environment maps can be used to edit the lighting effects of the face appearance. Unlike [Ramamoorthi and Hanrahan, 2001a], we do not need to know the face albedo.

1.2   Face relighting from a single image

Given a single photograph of a person's face, it is possible to approximate the radiance environment map, using the technique described in Section 2.1.3 of Chapter 6,

Given a photograph and a generic 3D face geometry, we first align the face image with the generic face model. Note that if the input image is a face texture image, it is already aligned with geometry. From the aligned photograph and the 3D geometry, we use the method described in Section 2.1.2 of Chapter 6 to approximate the radiance environment map. To relight the face image under rotated lighting environment, we compute each face pixel's normal (with respect to the lighting environment) before and after rotation. Then we compute ratio $\frac{I_{sphere}(\vec{n_b})}{I_{sphere}(\vec{n_a})}$, where $\vec{n_b}$ and $\vec{n_a}$ are the new and old normal vectors of the pixel respectively, and I_{sphere} is the approximated radiance environment map. Finally the new intensity of the pixel is given by equation (8.6).

If we are given photographs of two people's faces under different lighting conditions, we can modify the first photograph so that it matches the lighting condition of the second face. We first compute the radiance environment map for each face. If the two faces have the same average albedo, then the two radiance environment maps have the same albedo, and we can apply equation (8.11) to relight the first face to match the second face's lighting condition. In practice, if two people have similar skin colors, we can apply equation (8.11) to relight one face to match the lighting condition of the other.

Given one input face photograph and a user interface to edit the 9 coefficients of the radiance environment map, we can interactively synthesize novel illumination effects on the face image based on technique described in Section 1.1.4.

1.2.1 Dynamic range of images

Because digitized image has limited dynamic range, ratio-based relighting would have artifacts where skin pixel values are too low or nearly saturated. To alleviate the problem, we apply constrained texture synthesis for these pixels. Our assumption is that the high frequency face albeo, similar to texture, contains repetitive patterns. Thus we can infer local face appearance at the places of artifacts from examples on other part of the face. We first identify these pixels as outliers that do not satisfy Lambertian model using robust statistics [Hampel and *et. al*, 1986]. Then we use the remaining pixels as example to synthesize texture at the place of outliers. We use a patch-based Image Analogy algorithm [Hertzmann and et. al., 2001], with the constraint that a candidate patch should match the original patch up to a relighting scale factor. Since we use a patch-based approach and we only apply it to the detected outlier regions, the computation overhead is very small. Figure 8.1 shows an example where

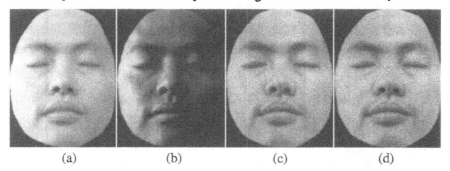

(a)   (b)   (c)   (d)

Figure 8.1. Using constrained texture synthesis to reduce artifacts in the low dynamic range regions. (a): input image; (b): blue channel of (a) with very low dynamic range; (c): relighting without synthesis; and (d): relighting with constrained texture synthesis.

the low dynamic range of the image causes artifacts in the relighting. (a) is the input image, whose blue channel (b) has very low intensity on the person's left face. (c) is the relighting result without using the constrained texture synthesis, and (d) is relighting result with constrained texture synthesis. We can see that almost all the unnatural color on the person's left face in (c) disappear in (d).

1.3   Implementation

In our implementations, we use a cyberware-scanned face mesh as our generic face geometry (shown in Figure 8.2(a)). All the examples reported in this paper are produced with this mesh. Given a 2D image, to create the correspondence between the vertices of the mesh and the 2D image, we first create the correspondence between the feature points on the mesh and the 2D image. The feature points on the 2D image are marked manually as shown in Figure 8.2(b). We are working on automatically detecting these facial features using techniques presented in [Hu et al., 2004]. We use image warping technique to generate the correspondence between the rest of the vertices on the mesh and the 2D image. A mapping from the image pixels to a radiometrically linear space is implemented to account for gamma correction. We have devel-

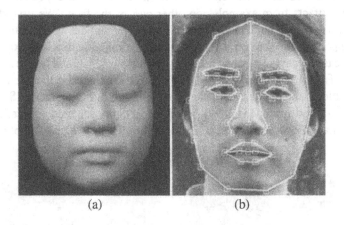

(a)   (b)

Figure 8.2.   (a): The generic mesh. (b): The feature points.

oped user interface for this face relighting software. It is illustrated in Figure 8.3. interactive light editing. The panel on the right is a control panel for controlling environment rotation, editing REM coefficients, and setting parameters such as the coefficient for gamma correction.

The computation of the radiance environment map takes about one second for a 640x480 input image on a PC with Pentium III 733 MHz and 512 MB memory. The face relighting is currently implemented completely in software without hardware acceleration. It runs about 10 frames per second.

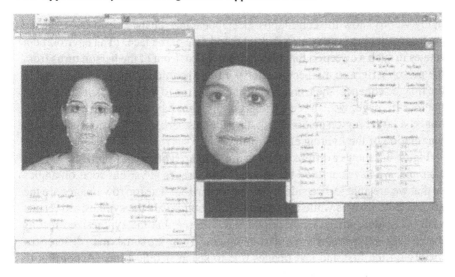

Figure 8.3. The user interface of the face relighting software.

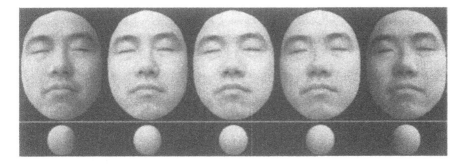

Figure 8.4. The middle image is the input. The sequence shows synthesized results of 180° rotation of the lighting environment.

1.4 Relighting results

We show some relighting experiment results on 2D face images in this section. The first example is shown in Figure 8.4 where the middle image is the input image. The radiance environment map is shown below the input image. It is computed by assuming the back is dark since the lights mostly come from the frontal directions. The rest of the images in the sequence show the relighting results when the lighting environment rotates. Below each image, we show the corresponding rotated radiance environment map. The environment rotates about 45° between each two images, a total of 180° rotation. The accompanying videos show the continuous face appearance changes, and the radiance environment map is shown on the righthand side of the face. (The environment rotates in such a direction that the environment in front of the person turns from the person's right to the person's left). From the middle image to the right in the image sequence, the frontal environment turns to the person's left side. On the fourth image, we can see that part of his right face gets darker. On the last image, a larger region on his right face becomes darker. This is consistent with the rotation of the lighting environment.

Figure 8.5 shows a different person in a similar lighting environment. For this example, we have captured the ground truth images at various rotation angles so that we are able to do a side-by-side comparison. The top row images are the ground truth images while the images at the bottom are the synthesized results with the middle image as the input. We can see that the synthesized results match very well with the ground truth images. There are some small differences mainly on the first and last images due to specular reflections (According to Marschner et al. [Marschner et al., 1999], human skin is almost Lambertian at small light incidence angles and has strong non-Lambertian scattering at higher angles).

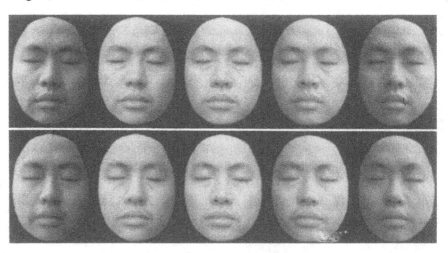

Figure 8.5.   The comparison of synthesized results and ground truth. The top row is the ground truth. The bottom row is synthesized result, where the middle image is the input.

The third example is shown in Figure 8.6. Again, the middle image is the input. In this example, the lights mainly come from two sides of the face. The bright white light on the person's right face comes from sky light and the reddish light on his left face comes from the sun light reflected by a red-brick building. The image sequence shows a 180° rotation of the lighting environment.

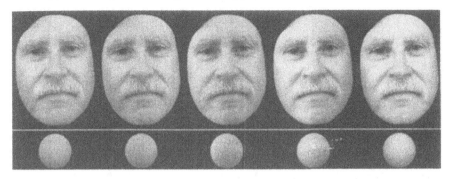

Figure 8.6. The middle image is the input. The sequence shows a 180° rotation of the lighting environment.

Figure 8.7 shows four examples of interactive lighting editing by modifying the spherical harmonics coefficients. For each example, the left image is the input image and the right image is the result after modifying the lighting. In example (a), lighting is changed to attach shadow on the person's left face. In example (b), the light on the person's right face is changed to be more reddish while the light on her left face becomes slightly more blueish. In (c), the bright sunlight move from the person's left face to his right face. In (d), we attach shadow to the person's right face and change the light color as well. Such editing would be difficult to do with the currently existing tools such as $Photoshop^{TM}$.

We have also experimented with our technique to relight a person's face to match the lighting condition on a different person's face image. As we pointed out in Section 1.2, our method can only be applied to two people with similar skin colors. In Figure 8.8(a), we relight a female's face shown on the left to match the lighting condition of a male shown in the middle. The synthesized result is shown on the right. Notice the darker region on the right face of the middle image. The synthesized result shows similar lighting effects. Figure 8.8(b) shows an example of relighting a male's face to a different male. Again, the left and middle faces are input images. The image on the right is the synthesized result. From the middle image, we can see that the lighting on his left face is a lot stronger than the lighting on his right face. We see similar lighting effects on the synthesized result. In addition, the dark region due to attached shadow on the right face of the synthesized image closely matches the shadow region on the right face of the middle image.

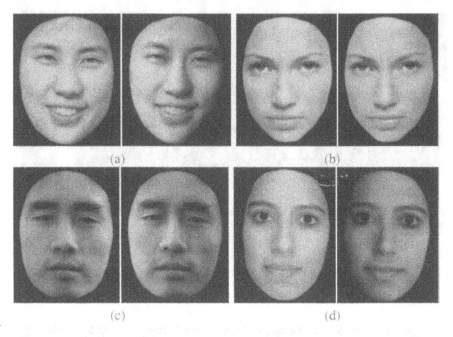

Figure 8.7. Interactive lighting editing by modifying the spherical harmonics coefficients of the radiance environment map.

2.   Face Relighting For Face Recognition in Varying Lighting

Face recognition has important applications in human computer interaction and security. Face recognition still remains a challenging problem because the performance of almost all current face recognition systems is heavily subject to the variations in the imaging conditions [Phillips et al., 2000], such as illumination variation.

In Section 1.3.1, we have reviewed approaches that have been proposed to deal with the illumination effects in face recognition. These approaches need either multiple training face image per person or 3D face model database for modeling illumination effects. Zhao and Chellappa [Zhao and R.Chellappa, 2000] tries to use only one image by recovering 3D shape from a single face image. They use symmetric shape-from-shading but the method may suffer from the drawbacks of shape-from-shading, such as the assumption of point lighting sources. Zhang and Samaras [Zhang and Samaras, 2003] propose to recover the 9 spherical harmonic basis images from a single face image. The method in [Zhang and Samaras, 2003] needs a 3D database as in [Blanz et al., 2002] to estimate a statistical model of the spherical harmonic basis images.

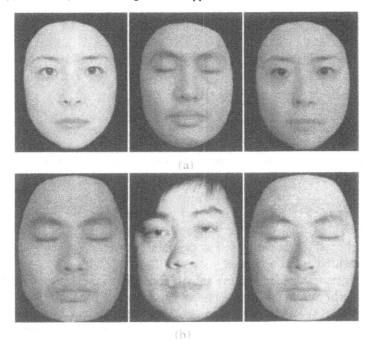

Figure 8.8.   Relighting under different lighting. For both (a) and (b): Left: Face to be relighted. Middle: target face. Right: result.

In this section, we show that our technique on face relighting from a single image can be used for face recognition. The advantage of this approach is that it only require one image for modeling illumination effects. The underline theory of this technique holds under general lighting conditions, such as area light sources.

To normalize the illumination effects for face recognition, we propose to relight all face images into one canonical lighting condition. The lighting condition of the training images can be used as the canonical lighting condition. Then we can use equation 8.11 for relighting images into the canonical lighting condition. After that, any face recognition algorithms such as Eigenfaces (PCA) [Turk and Pentland, 1991], Fisherfaces (LDA) [Belhumeur et al., 1997], can be used on the pre-processed face images for face recognition.

In our preliminary experiments, we first test our approach using the public available face database: "Yale Face Database B" [Georghiades et al., 2001]. The database contains 5760 single light source images of 10 subjects each seen under 576 viewing conditions (9 poses × 64 illumination conditions). In our current experiment, we only consider illumination variations so that we choose to perform face recognition for the 640 frontal pose images. We choose the

Figure 8.9.   Examples of Yale face database B [Georghiades et al., 2001]. From left to right, they are images from group 1 to group 5.

simplest image correlation as the similarity measure between two images, and nearest neighbor as the classifier. For the 10 subjects in the database, we take only one frontal image per person as the training image. The remaining 630 images are used as testing image.

The images are divided into five subsets according to the angles of the light source direction from the camera optical axis. For the five subset, the values of angle are: (1) less than 12 degrees; (2) between 12 and 25 degrees; (3) between 25 and 50 degrees; (4) between 50 and 77 degrees; and (5) larger than 77 degrees. The face images in the Yale database contain challenging examples for relighting. For example, there are many images with strong cast shadows; or with saturated or extremely low intensity pixel values Figure 8.9 shows one sample image per group of the Yale face database B.

We compare the recognition results using original images and relighted images. The experimental results are shown in Figure 8.10. We can see that the recognition error rates are reduced after face relighting in all the cases. When the lighting angles become larger, the illumination effects in original test images are more different from the training images. Therefore, the recognition error rates become larger. In these scenarios, our relighting technique significantly reduces the error rates, even in very extreme conditions (e.g. lighting angles larger than 77 degrees).

In summary, our face relighting technique provides an efficient and effective way to normalize the illumination effects for face recognition. Compared to other approaches, this method has the following advantages: (1) it does not assume simple point lighting source model; instead it works under natural illumination in the real world; (2) it only needs one training image per person to model illumination effects without the need of multiple training images or 3D face database. In the future, we plan to further improve the results under extreme lighting conditions. To deal with cast shadows, techniques using more basis images such as that in [Debevec et al., 2000] will be useful. The difference between the 3D generic face geometry and the actual one may introduce artifacts. We are planning on estimating a personalized geometric model from

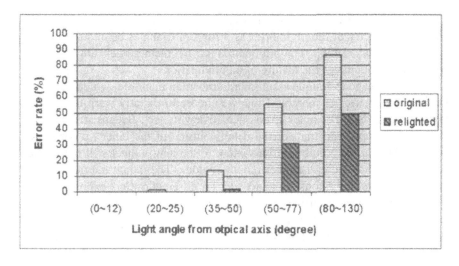

Figure 8.10. Recognition error rate comparison of before relighting and after relighting on the Yale face database.

the input image by using techniques such as those reported in [Blanz and Vetter, 1999, Zhang et al., 2001].

3. Synthesize Appearance Details of Facial Motion

Liu et al. [Liu et al., 2001a] used ratio image technique, called Expression Ratio Image (ERI), to map one person's face expression details to other people's faces. More generally, this technique can be used to synthesize facial-motion-related appearance variations for new subject. In this way, the appearance examples for visemes and expressions can be used in face synthesis for new people. In this section, we discuss two issues that need extra consideration when applying the ratio image technique. First we discuss how to map appearance of mouth interior in Section 3.1. The mouth interior appearance is important for applications such as lip-reading, but does not satisfy the assumption of ratio image technique. Next, We describe how to create face animations with appearance variations in Section 3.2.

3.1 Appearance of mouth interior

The appearance of teeth and tongue is important for visual speech perception. However, there is no robust technique to capture their motion so far. Moreover, compared to the skin it is more difficult to measure the surface reflectance property for realistic rendering. Due to these reasons, it is more feasible to capture the motion details of mouth interior using appearance.

To use texture variation to synthesize the mouth interior motion, we simplify the geometry of mouth interior as 3 rows of triangles behind the lips as in [Guenter et al., 1998]. The original tongue and teeth models are still used when we do not change the texture of mouth interior.

The ratio image technique assumes a Lambertian manifold, which does not hold for the interior of mouth. Thus, we choose to directly warp the mouth interior texture based on inner lip contours to new subject. Because ratio image technique is applied to transfer the details outside of the inner lip contours, copying the warped mouth interior texture to the new subject will not create sharp discrepancy along the inner mouth contour. The mouth interior texture can be modulated by a constant to account for different camera exposure.

In a preliminary experiment with 2D face images, we map one person's speech-related appearance variations in mouth area to a different person. The results are illustrated in Figure 8.11.

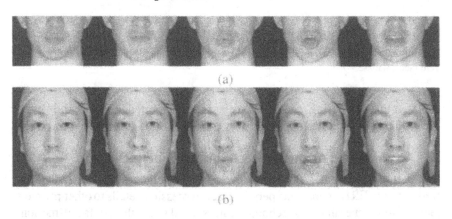

Figure 8.11. Mapping visemes of (a) to (b). For (b), the first neutral image is the input, the other images are synthesized.

3.2 Linear alpha-blending of texture

To synthesize face texture variation caused by facial motion, we use linear combinations of face appearance examples. This idea of multi-texture blending has been shown to be useful in facial motion synthesis by Pighin et al. [Pighin et al., 1998] and Reveret et al. [Reveret and Essa, 2001]. Furthermore, it is well supported by graphics hardware. For a face appearance example set $\{I_k, k = 1...K\}$, we represent an arbitrary texture as

$$\hat{I} = \sum_{k=1}^{K} w_k I_k \qquad (8.12)$$

In Chapter 5, we have discussed how to generate face animations using geometric MUs. To augment the synthesis with appearance variations, we propose to decide the texture blending coefficients based on the corresponding geometric MUPs. The intuition is that geometry and appearance are correlated such that partial information about appearance can be inferred from the corresponding geometry. In similar spirit, Zhang et al. [Zhang et al., 2003] have demonstrated the effectiveness of synthesizing facial expression appearance details from given geometry.

Compared to [Zhang et al., 2003], the geometry part of motion is fully derived from our geometric-model-based synthesis. Thus we can design a simpler formulation for the blending coefficients. In this scenario, the problem is to find an appropriate texture given geometric shape: s. Suppose the corresponding geometric MUP is $\vec{c}(\mathbf{s})$ and the exemplars' geometric MUPs are $\{\vec{c}_k, k = 1...K\}$. We define the blending the coefficient as

$$w(\mathbf{s}) = be^{-\lambda_k \|\vec{c}(\mathbf{s}) - \vec{c}_k\|^2} \tag{8.13}$$

where b is a constant which normalize the sum of blending coefficients to 1. In practice, we need to avoid the blurring of the blending result. For this purpose, we adjust the value of the constant λ_k experimentally such that there are only $N, (N < K)$ nonzero blending coefficients. Other coefficients are small and can be set to zero.

4. Summary

We have described methods of face synthesis based on the flexible appearance model. In particular, we have discussed two issues: (1) how to synthesize illumination effects in face appearance; and (2) how to synthesize appearance variations in face animations. The main contribution of this chapter is that we show that our flexible appearance model can be used for synthesis in a flexible way. More specifically, It means we can synthesize appearance variations based on the model across different people and illumination environments.

Chapter 9

APPLICATION EXAMPLES OF THE FACE PROCESSING FRAMEWORK

In this chapter, we discuss applications of our 3D face processing framework. Two application will be described in more details. The first application is model-based very low bit-rate face video coding. The other application is an integrated human-computer interaction environment. Finally, we conclude this chapter and discuss other potential applications that could benefit from our 3D face processing framework.

1. Model-based Very Low Bit-rate Face Video Coding

1.1 Introduction

Facial motions convey very important visual cues which are valuable for human-to-human communication. When the volume of video data is overwhelming and stable high-capacity bandwidth is not available, very low bit rate video coding can be a solution for teleconferencing.

To accommodate the needs of transmission of large volume of video data over limited channel, several video coding standards, such as MPEG-1, MPEG-2, H.261, H.263 and H.264 have been proposed. Because these approaches only utilize the spatial-temporal redundancy statistics of the video waveform signal without a prior knowledge of the semantic content of the video, they are well applicable for general purpose video data compression where the scene in video frame is arbitrary. In the mean time, due to the difficulty to extract redundancy from video, a high coding rate usually also accompanies a high coding latency for certain video quality. This hinders these approaches from applications where real-time video transmission is needed.

For the applications where human face is known as the major focus of attention, model-based coding has been proposed to improve coding efficiency [Aizawa and Huang, 1995]. One example is the MPEG-4 face animation standard [MPEG4, 1997]. In these approaches, the human face geometry is characterized with a 3D mesh model. The facial motion is parameterized as rotation and translation for rigid motion, and action unit or facial muscle weights for non-rigid facial motions. These parameters together with the video background can be transmitted over channel at very low bit rate, and the video can be reconstructed via synthesis of the facial area based on the transmitted parameters. However, currently there are no completely model-based available coder yet, because it is difficult to extract these facial geometry and motion parameters from video automatically and robustly. Furthermore, the residual of the model-based coding is not transmitted in many approaches. Therefore, the differences between the original video and reconstructed video could be arbitrarily large.

Eisert et al. [Eisert et al., 2000] propose a hybrid coding technique using a model-based 3D facial motion tracking algorithm. In this approach, the model-based coding results and waveform-based coding results are compared and best results are used. In this way, the two coding schemes can complement each other. In this book, we propose a model-based face video coder in similar spirit. Nonetheless, the proposed very low bit rate face coding method is efficient and robust because of our 3D face tracking.

We first locate the face in the video frame. Next, the generic facial geometric model is adapted to the face, and facial texture for the model is extracted from the first frame of the video. The facial motion is then tracked and synthesized. The residual error in face area and video background are then coded with state-of-the-art waveform based coder. Finally the facial motion parameters, coded residual error and video background are transmitted at very low bit rate. Experiments show that our method can achieve better PSNR around facial area than the state-of-the-art waveform-based video coder at about the same low bit rate. Moreover, our proposed face video coder has better subjective visual effects.

1.2   Model-based face video coder

The face video is first sent to a face tracker that extracts face motion parameters. Then a face synthesizer synthesize a face appearance based on the motion parameters. After the synthesized face is obtained, the residual error can be calculated by subtracting it from the original frame. The video frame is divided into foreground residual and background region. For the background and foreground residual, since we do not assume prior knowledge about it we can employ the advantage of state-of-the-art waveform-based coder to do the coding. The advantage of this approach is that the facial motion details not captured by the geometric motion parameters will not be lost when the video is coded at the low bit rate.

The chosen waveform-based video coder is JVT reference software JM 4.2 obtained from [H26L, 2002]. It is a joint effort between ISO MPEG and ITU H.26x after the successful H.264 development, and represents the state-of-the-

	Face Video Coder	H.264/JVT Coder
Bit-rate	18-19 Kbps	
PSNR	29.28	27.35
Coding Time	1.4	5

Table 9.1. Performance comparisons between the face video coder and H.264/JVT coder.

art in low bitrate video coding. The background will be coded as ordinary video frames by H.264/JVT codec, and the foreground residuals are coded by $Intra\_16X16$ mode of the H.264/JVT coder. At receiver, the decoder synthesizes the facial motion according to the received face motion parameters, reconstructs the foreground and background regions, and recovers the foreground facial area by summing up the synthesized face and transmitted foreground residuals. Because most of the facial motion details are captured by the facial motion parameters, the foreground residual tends to have small amplitude, we can choose to code the video with very lot bit rates without losing much information of the foreground.

For the face tracker in the system, we used the geometric 3D face tracking system described in Chapter 4. The face synthesizer uses the methods presented in Chapter 5. In the current model-based face video coder, we ignore the face texture variations in tracker and synthesizer. Instead, we let H.264/JVT coder to deal with them. In the future, we plan to apply our flexible appearance model to deal with these texture variations.

1.3 Results

The face tracker runs on a PC with two $Pentium^{TM}4$ 2.2GHZ processors, G-Force 4 video card, and 2G memories. With only one processor employed, the tracking system can reach 25 frame per second (fps) in rigid tracking mode and 14 fps in non-rigid tracking mode. We capture and encode videos of 352×240 at 30Hz. At the same low bit-rate ($18 \sim 19$ kbits/s), we compare this hybrid coding with H.26L JM 4.2 reference software. For a face video sequence with 147 frames, the performance comparisons of the two coders are presented in Table 9.1. It can be observed that our face video coder has higher Peak Signal to Noise Ratio (PSNR) for face area and is more computationally efficient. Figure 9.1 shows three snapshots of a video with 147 frames. One important result is that our face video coder results have much higher visual quality in face area.

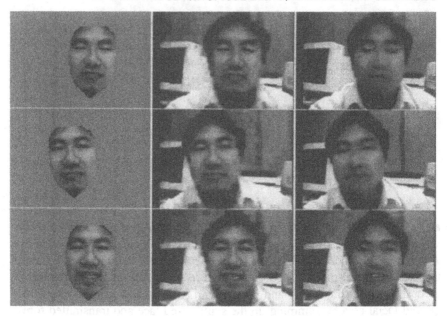

Figure 9.1. (a) The synthesized face motion. (b) The reconstructed video frame with synthesized face motion. (c) The reconstructed video frame using H.26L codec.

1.4   Summary and future work

As an application of the 3D face processing framework, we present an efficient and robust very low bit rate face coding method via 3D face face tracking. The facial motion parameters can be extracted from the video and transmitted over the channel. Then the facial area residual errors and video background can be coded using waveform-based coder at very low bit rates. Experiments show that our method can achieve better PSNR around facial area than H.264/JVT coder at about the same low bit rate and have better subjective visual quality.

The key issue of model-based coding is the 3D face tracker. We plan to improve the accuracy and robustness of our 3D face tracking algorithm. Because our tracking system works in real-time, we can combine it with real-time waveform-based coder to make the overall system real-time. Then it could be used in a real-time low bit-rate video phone application. Finally, we plan to model the face texture variation so that the residual can be further reduced.

2.   Integrated Proactive HCI environments

Face tracking and expression recognition techniques help computers monitor users' states in a human-computer interaction (HCI) environments. On the other hand, the face synthesis technique can be used to create synthetic avatar to interact with users. Here we describe an integrated HCI environment where our face processing techniques are used.

2.1 Overview

In the Beckman Institute for Advanced Science and Technology at the University of Illinois at Urbana-Champaign, there is an interdisciplinary project called: "Multimodal Human Computer Interaction: Towards a Proactive Computer". The goal of the project is to (1) identify ways to provide the computer with real-time information about the human user's cognitive, motivational and emotional state; and (2) explore ways of making the computer take actions proactively based on the states information. In this way, the computer will no long only take commands from the user passively. Instead, it will initiate actions based on user's states and thus make the human-computer interaction more effectively.

The current application area for the project is science education, in which children learn about the properties of gears via $LEGO^{TM}$ games. By learning how to put gears together, the children can learn scientific principles about ratio, forces and etc. The educational philosophy is su   that learning through exploration is valued. That is, rather than directing the child in carrying out learning tasks, the goal is to (1) encourage exploration of gears and gear trains in which principles of gears are learned; and (2) ask questions that encourage thought and insight. The final goal is a HCI learning environment that engages children in activities with the tasks, tracks their path and progress in the problem space, and initiates communication (e.g. asking questions, making comments, showing examples, etc.). These activities will then encourage exploration, maintain and develop interest and move the child toward new understandings.

In this learning environment, the information exchanged among different participants is multimodal. The computer is used to analyze the multimodel input, including facial expression analysis, prosody analysis, context-based word spotting, visual tracking of the task states and eye-gaze tracking. Based on the multimodal input analysis, the computer can estimate the user states. Then the computer can map the user states to actions to be taken. The mapping can be designed by domain expert or learned from extensive examples. Finally, the computer executes the action to guide the children in the next step of exploration. One type of useful output from the computer is synthetic face animation. The synthetic face avatar can be used to represent the computer to interact with children and help engage user in the learning session.

2.2   Current status

Initially, human tutoring sessions with children were videotaped and extensively analyzed. As a result a set of annotated tapes and transcripts are produced. These collected data may serve as input to computer learning algorithms that are attempting to establish a mapping from user's states information to tutor actions.

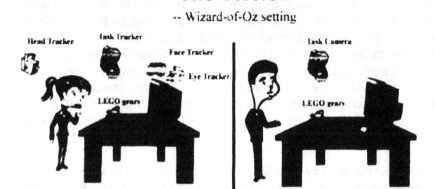

Figure 9.2.   The setting for the Wizard-of-Oz experiments.

Currently, the integrative human-computer interaction control system is being developed. The results of the multimodal input and output are displayed for the sessions operating in a Wizard-of-Oz environment. The environment is illustrated in Figure 9.2. In this environment, the child and the tutor are in separate rooms. The student is not aware of the presence of a human tutor. Instead, the child supposes he or she is interacting with the computer via the face avatar. The avatar outputs synthesized speech, shows emotional expression and directs the student's gaze to selected regions. Meanwhile their behaviors are recorded for further study. On the other hand the instructor can see the multimodal signal analysis results and initiate appropriate actions. The interfaces for the child and the instructor are shown in Figure 9.3. This system is currently being used in educational/psychological research. Experimenting are being carried out to classify multimodal input into user state categories. The classification is beginning to replace manual analysis of some video data.

As shown in Figure 9.3, 3D face tracing and expression recognition techniques are now used as part of the cues to estimate the states information. Other useful cues include speech prosody, states of the task, and etc. On the other hand, the synthetic face animation is used as the avatar to interact with the

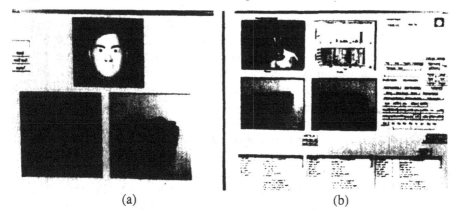

Figure 9.3. (a) The interface for the student. (b) The interface for the instructor.

child. Preliminary results suggest that the synthetic avatar helps the children more patient in the learning session.

2.3 Future work

In this proactive HCI environment, the facial motions of the children are very challenging to analyze compared to database collected in controlled laboratory conditions. One reason is that real facial motions tend to be very fast at certain occasions. These fast motions can cause the current face tracker lose track. In the future, we need to future improve the speed of the face tracker so that it can capture fast facial motions in real-life conditions. Another reason is that real facial expressions observed in real-life environment are more subtle. Therefore, the performance of the face expression recognition can be affected. We plan to carry out extensive studies of facial expression classification using face video data with spontaneous expressions. In this process, we could be able to improve the expression classifier.

Another future direction of improvements is to make the synthetic face avatar more active so that it can better engage the children in the exploration. For example, we plan to synthesize head movements and facial expressions in the context of task states and user states. In this way, the avatar can be more lifelike and responsive to users' actions in the interaction. One possible direction is explore the correlation of speech and head movements as the work by Graf et al. [Graf et al., 2002].

3. Summary

In this chapter, we have described two applications of our 3D face processing framework. One application is to use face processing techniques to encode face visual cues in communication. Experiment shows that this approach achieves higher PSNR and better visual quality in very low bit-rate conditions. The other application is an integrated HCI environment for computer-aided education. In this environment, face analysis techniques is used to understand the users' state and synthetic face is used as interface to help engage users.

More generally, our face processing framework can be applied in many applications related to human faces. Besides the two applications described in this chapter, other examples of potential applications include: (1) intelligent video surveillance; and (2) diagnosis and rehabilitation tools for face-related medical problems. In security-related video surveillance, human faces provide valuable visual cues to identify people and understand human activities. In face-related medical problems, such as disorders of facial muscles and associated nervous system, facial visual cues are important input for diagnosis of the problems. Our face processing framework provides a possibility for automating the diagnosis. On the other hand, one of the rehabilitation techniques is presenting appropriate audio-visual stimuli (e.g. videos of normal facial expressions and talking faces) to patients. The face synthesis techniques can help to generate and manipulate these stimuli more easily.

Chapter 10

CONCLUSION AND FUTURE WORK

In this book, we have presented a unified 3D face processing framework. Various aspects of face processing research have been discussed in the context of multi-modal human computer interaction and intelligent video analysis. In this chapter, we summarize the contributions of this book and outline the future research directions.

1. Conclusion

In this book, we have presented a unified 3D face processing framework. In Chapter 2, we describe tools for building 3D geometric models of neutral faces. Using these tools, we can create personalized 3D face models for 3D face tracking and animation. Then we discuss the geometric facial motion models in the framework in Chapter 3. These motion models are derived from motion capture data of real face motions. Thus they can capture the characteristics of real face motions. After that, we present our approaches for 3D non-rigid face tracking and animation in Chapter 4 and Chapter 5, respectively. We demonstrate the efficacy of tracking and animation, using experimental results in very low bit-rate face video coding, speech-drive face animation, and etc.

In Chapter 6, we present flexible appearance model to deal with appearance details which are lost in the geometric facial motion models. In out experiments, these details are shown to be important for computer analysis of subtle facial expressions [Wen and Huang, 2003], and human perception of synthesized face animations [Wen et al., 2003]. Compared to most existing appearance models for face motions, our flexible appearance model is less illumination dependent, and less person-dependent. It also requires less data for estimating the parameters of the flexible appearance model. Therefore, our appearance model can be more flexibly used in various environments.

2.   Future Work

To improve the 3D face processing framework, future research should be conducted in the following several directions.

2.1   Improve geometric face processing

The geometric face processing can be improved by utilizing more statistics of increasingly available 3D face data. One direction is to estimate better 3D face geometry from a single face image following the approach of Blanz and Vetter [Blanz and Vetter, 1999]. The improved 3D face estimation can provide a better 3D-model-fitting for the first video frame in the non-rigid face tracking. The more accurate 3D face model will also improve the performance of face relighting techniques described in Section 1 of Chapter 8.

Another direction is to collect motion capture data of more subjects so that the model derived from data can better describe the variations across different people. As a result, facial motion analysis can be used for a larger variety of people. For synthesis, such database would enable the study the personalized styles in visual speech or facial expression synthesis.

2.2   Closer correlation between geometry and appearance

In our current 3D face processing framework, we first use geometric model to process the geometric-level motion. Next, the remaining appearance details are handled by the flexible appearance model. In this procedure, we assume that the geometric processing part gives reasonable results so that face textures are correctly aligned with the geometry. However, this assumption is not always true. For example, in 3D face motion analysis, if the geometric tracking gets lost, the extracted face texture would be wrong and the appearance-based analysis would then fail.

One solution for dealing this problem is to derive constraints of geometric tracking from appearance models. La Cascia et al. [Cascia et al., 2000] model the face with a texture-mapped cylinder. The constraint is that the face image should be a projection of the texture-mapped cylinder. 3D rigid face tracking was formulated as a texture image registration problem, in which the global rotation and translation parameters of the cylinder are estimated. Recently, Vacchetti et al. [Vacchetti et al., 2003] use the face appearances in a few key frames and the preceding frame as constraints for estimating the 3D rigid geometric face motions. These constraints help to reduce drifting and jittering, even when there are large out-of-plane rotations and partial occlusions. In these methods, the texture variation models serve to constrain the feasible solution space of the geometric tracking. Thus the robustness of the geometric tracking can be improved. This leads to more robust appearance-based motion analysis which is based on the geometric tracking results. In other words, a closer coupling of the geometry and appearance processing improves the overall performance.

To improve our face processing, we plan to investigate closer correlations between geometry and appearance, following the direction mentioned in [Cascia et al., 2000] and [Vacchetti et al., 2003]. In our current geometric tracking algorithm, template-matching based optical-flow is used to estimate the frame to frame motions. To alleviate the error accumulation (i.e. drifting) problem of long term template-matching, it uses the templates from the previous frames and the first frames. For example, the even nodes of the face mesh is tracked using templates from the previous frame and the odd nodes are tracked using templates from the first frame. However, only the templates in the first frame and the previous frame do not give a sufficient description of the appearance variations of the templates. Therefore, the tracking is not accurate when the out-of-plane rotation angle is large (e.g. larger than 40 degrees). In the future, we plan to adopt better statistical models of the templates by (1) deriving statistical models offline using rendering of 3D face databases; (2) adopting the novel appearance features proposed in Chapter 7 that are less illumination and person dependent; and (3) online adaptation of the models using approaches suggested by [Jepson et al., 2001]. Then these models of template appearance can be used to improve the robustness of geometric tracking under large 3D pose variations, partial occlusions and etc.

2.3   Human perception evaluation of synthesis

Human perception evaluation of face synthesis should be done in the context of specific applications such as lip reading. Hypotheses about visual factors need be created and tested in the evaluation. These hypotheses can then be used to improve face synthesis so that the synthetic animation can be more effective for applications.

2.3.1   Previous work

To evaluate the quality of synthetic face animation, one approach is to compare the synthetic face with the original face in terms of reconstructed error. This approach is used by (1) low bit-rate coding oriented face animation such as MPEG-4 FAPs [Eisert et al., 2000, Tu et al., 2003]; and (2) machine learning-based data-driven face animation such as [Brand, 1999, Guenter et al., 1998].

However, the synthetic face motion can be different from the real motion but still looks natural. Consequently, human subject evaluations are important. Human evaluation with a small set of subjects were used in [Brand, 1999, Ezzat et al., 2002]. On the other hand, in many scenarios mimicking real human face motion is not the only goal for synthetic face animation. For example, non photo-realistic styles and abstraction can be created to convey certain information in face animation [Buck and et al., 2000, Chen et al., 2002]. Another type of face animation applications is emerging from the interdisciplinary Human Computer Interaction research areas, such as using synthetic face animation for language training [Cole et al., 1999] and psychological studies [Massaro, 1998]. For these scenarios, the naturalness of face animation can be compromised, while certain motions can be exaggerated for application purpose (e.g. mouth motion for lip-reading applications). Therefore, human subject perception experiments are usually carried out within the application context, to evaluate and guide further improvement of the face animation. Massro et al. [Massaro, 1998] have developed a face modeling and animation system, called "Baldi". "Baldi" has been used to generate synthetic stimuli for bimodal speech perception research. Moreover, it has been applied in language training for school children [Cole et al., 1999].

For multi-modal human speech perception, a 3-process model was proposed by Massro et al. [Massaro, 1998]. The three processes are: (1) "evaluation", which transforms the sources of information to features; (2) "integration", where multiple features are integrated both between modalities and within a modality; and (3) "decision", which makes perception decision based on integration results. For integration, a Fuzzy Logical Model of Perception (FLMP) was proposed. It is mathematically equivalent to Bayes' theorem, which is widely used in pattern recognition. FLMP has been shown to be effective in integrating multiple cues for multi-modal speech perception.

"Baldi" and the FLMP model were used to test hypotheses on bimodal speech perception. Some important results include:

- The auditory and visual channels could be asynchronous to certain degrees without affecting the performance of speech perception. In Massro's work, $100 \sim 200$ ms delays of one channel did not interfere with the performance. Some words/phonemes allow longer delays than the others. This result agrees with other researchers' findings. McGrath and Summerfield [McGrath and Summerfield, 1985] reported that a delay up to 80 ms did not disrupt performance. Pandey, Kunov and Abel [Pandey et al., 1986] found an upper limit of 120 ms. A result of 200 ms as the upper limit was reported by Campbell and Dodd [Campbell and Dodd, 1980].

- The speech reading performances are relatively robust under various conditions, including different peripheral views, image resolution, viewing angles and distances. First, experiments show that speech reading performances do not degrade even when the perceiver is not looking directly at the mouth. Second, as the resolution of face image decreases, phonemes with large scale motion such as /W/ can still be reliably recognized. However, phoneme featuring more detailed motion such as the interdental motion of /TH/, can get confused with other phonemes. Next, it is also found that speech reading performances degrade little when viewing non frontal faces. Profile views even improve performances for certain phonemes. But on the average, frontal views are still the best. Finally, the performances remain fairly good, when the distance from the synthetic talker to the perceiver is within 4 meters.

Other researchers also reported that speechreading is robust when dynamics of visual speech is changed. IJsseldijk [IJsseldijk, 1992] found that performance speechreading degraded little even when the temporal sequence is slowed down four times. Williams and et al. [Williams et al., 1997] reported that the recognition rates of visemes degraded less than 5%, even when the sampling rate of visual speech was only $5 \sim 10$ frame per second.

- It is also reported that adding extra visual features could improve speech reading after a few rounds of training. For example, in their experiments color bars were used to show whether the current sound is "nasal", "voicing" or "friction". The bars were displayed besides the talking face. The results showed that speech reading correct rates improved significantly after presenting the material five times to the perceivers. It implies that perceivers could adapt to the extra visual features in a fairly short period of time.

Although "Baldi" has been shown to be a useful animation tools for research and applications in speechreading, it has the following limitations:

- Only macrostructure level geometric motions are modeled in current system. Therefore, it loses important visual cues such as the shading changes of the lips and area within the mouth. These visual cues are important to perceive lip gestures such as rounding and retraction, and relative positions of articulators such as teeth and tongue. As a result, subtle phonemes (e.g. /R/) are more easily confused. To deal with this problem, one possible way is to use significantly more detailed geometry and advanced rendering to reproduce these subtle appearance changes. Modeling detailed geometric motion of mouth can be very expensive, because it involves complex wrinkles, surface discontinuities and non-rigid self collisions. Furthermore, the mouth interior is difficult to measure. For real-time rendering, it is also expensive to model the diverse material properties of lip, teeth and tongue and perform ray-tracing. Therefore, modeling these visual cues as texture variation is more feasible for speech perception applications.

- "Baldi" is a complex animation system with a great number of parameters. For basic tongue movement alone, there are more then 30 parameters. If a user wants to create customized face shapes for applications, it would be difficult and time-consuming unless the user has in-depth knowledge of "Baldi". Therefore, it is desired that systematic approaches be developed to simplify the use of the animation system. For example, one possible systematic approach could be to customize the face shapes from real data using machine learning techniques.

- The development of "Baldi" is not based on an open framework. That is, the components, such as spatial deformation model and temporal deformation model, are created and tuned exclusively for "Baldi". Therefore, it is difficult for other researchers to incorporate components of "Baldi" into other animation systems. It would be highly desirable that the development of "Baldi" is formulated as more general methodology such that other researchers could re-use and refine its components in the future.

2.3.2   Our ongoing and future work

Compared to "Baldi", one of the goals of our research is to provide a general, unified framework to guide the development of face motion modeling, analysis and synthesis. It could result in compact and efficient animation tools, which can be used by users with various backgrounds (e.g. psychologists) to create animation suitable for their applications. On the other hand, we make use of feedback from those applications to devise general principles to guide the refinement of the synthesis.

The current target application for evaluating our face synthesis is lip-reading. In this application, face animations synchronized with speech are generated and presented to hearing-impaired people. If the face animations are lip-readable, it will help the hearing-impaired people better understand the speech. We plan to conduct human perception studies to identify hypotheses about visual factors that are important to lip-reading. Then these hypotheses can be used to guide the improvement of the face synthesis.

In our preliminary experiments, we first create animations for isolated digits. Then these animations are presented to human subjects. The current subjects include one PhD student and one faculty member who have lip-reading experiences. In the first test, we test the lip-readability of face animation produced using geometric motion model only. We find the following factors limit the lip-readability: (1) the animation lacks wrinkles and shading changes in lip area so that it is difficult for the perception of lip rounding and protrusion when their durations are small; (2) the crafted tongue and teeth motions do not provide enough visual cues to recognize interdental phoneme like $/TH/$ in "three". Besides, certain un-natural synthesis results of mouth interior are distracting for lip-reading. In the second test, we augment the animation by using appearance model to synthesize texture variation. The results show that the perception of subtle lip rounding, protrusion and stretching is considerably improved because of the added appearance variations. The appearance model also handles the complex details inside the mouth. As a result, the recognition of interdental phonemes such as $/TH/$ is improved. However, subtle dynamic appearance changes, such as the fast tongue tip movement in "nine", can not by synthesized by the appearance model. The reason is that only one image is currently used to model a phoneme, thus the dynamic details are lost.

In the future, we plan to conduct human perception test using more subjects so that the experiment results can be more statistically rigorous. We need to identify people whose visual speeches are highly lip-readable, and derive better motion models from their data (both geometrical and appearance model). We also plan to investigate methods using increased appearance samples to model the dynamic appearance changes.

Appendix A
Projection of face images in 9-D spherical harmonic space

The multiplication of two spherical harmonic basis satisfies the following relation according to [Cohen-Tannoudji and et al., 1977]:

$$Y_{l_1 m_1}(\vec{n}) Y_{l_2 m_2}(\vec{n}) = \sum_{l=|l_1-l_2|}^{l_1-l_2} \sum_{m=-l}^{l} \{ C\langle l_1, l_2 : 0, 0 | l, 0 \rangle$$
$$\cdot C\langle l_1, l_2 : m_1, m_2 | l, m \rangle Y_{lm}(\vec{n}) \} \tag{A.1}$$

where $C\langle l_1, l_2 : m_1, m_2 | l, m \rangle$ is the Clebsch-Gordan coefficients. The coefficient of $Y_{lm}(\vec{n})$ in the righthand side is non-zero if and only if $m = m_1 + m_2$, l range from $|l_1 - l_2|$ to $l_1 + l_2$ and $l_1 + l_2 - l$ is even.

We then look at the second term of the righthand side in equation 6.7. Suppose $Y_{l_1 m_1}(\vec{n})$ comes from $\Psi(\vec{n})$, and $Y_{l_2 m_2}(\vec{n})$ comes from the factor corresponding to lighting. For any $Y_{l_2 m_2}(\vec{n})$, we have $0 \leq l_2 \leq 2$. If $l_1 > 4$ for any $Y_{l_1 m_1}(\vec{n})$, we have $l \geq |l_1 - l_2| > 2$. That proves the claim that if $\Psi(\vec{n})$ does not have the first four order ($l = 1, 2, 3, 4$) components, the second term of the righthand side in equation 6.7 contains components with orders equal to or higher than 3.

References

[Adini et al., 1997] Adini, Y., Moses, Y., and Ullman, S. (1997). Face recognition: The problem of compensating for changes in illumination derection. *IEEE Transaction on Pattern Analysis and Machine Intelligence*, 19:721–732.

[Aizawa and Huang, 1995] Aizawa, K. and Huang, T. S. (1995). Model-based image coding. *Proc. IEEE*, 83:259–271.

[Akimoto et al., 1993] Akimoto, T., Suenaga, Y., and Wallace, R. S. (1993). Automatic 3d facial models. *IEEE Computer Graphics and Applications*, 13(5):16–22.

[Badler and Platt, 1981] Badler, N. and Platt, S. (1981). Animating facial expressions. In *Computer Graphics*, pages 245–252. Siggraph.

[Bartlett et al., 1999] Bartlett, M. S., Hager, J. C., Ekman, P., and Sejnowski, T. J. (1999). Measuring facial expressions by computer image analysis. *Psychophysiology*, pages 253–263.

[Basri and Jacobs, 2001] Basri, R. and Jacobs, D. (2001). Lambertian reflectance and linear subspaces. In *International Conference on Computer Vision (ICCV'01)*, pages 383–390.

[Basu et al., 1998] Basu, S., Oliver, N., and Pentland, A. (1998). 3d modeling and tracking of human lip motions. In *International Conference on Computer Vision (ICCV'98)*, pages 337–343.

[Belhumeur et al., 1997] Belhumeur, P., Hespanha, J., and Kriegman, D. (1997). Eigenfaces vs. fisherfaces: Recognition using class specific linear projection. *IEEE Transaction on Pattern Analysis and Machine Intelligence*, pages 711–720.

[Belhumeur and Kriegman, 1998] Belhumeur, P. and Kriegman, D. (1998). What is the set of images of an object under all possible lighting conditions. *International Journal of Computer Vision*, 28(3):245–260.

[Beymer and Poggio, 1996] Beymer, D. and Poggio, T. (1996). Image representation for visual learning. *Science*, 272:1905–1909.

[Bishop, 1995] Bishop, C. M. (1995). *Neural Networks for Pattern Recognition*. Clarendon Press.

[Black and Yacoob, 1995] Black, M. J. and Yacoob, Y. (1995). Tracking and recognizing rigid and non-rigid facial motions using local parametric models of image motions. In *International Conference on Computer Vision*, pages 374–381.

[Blake et al., 1993] Blake, A., Cuiwen, R., and Zisserman, A. (1993). Affine-invariant contour tracking with automatic control of spatiotemporal scale. In *International Conference on Computer Vision*, pages 66–75.

[Blake et al., 1995] Blake, A., Isard, M. A., and Reynard, D. (1995). Learning to track the visual motion of contours. *Artificial Intelligence*, 78:101–134,.

[Blanz et al., 2002] Blanz, V., Romdhani, S., and Vetter, T. (2002). Face identification across different poses and illumination with a 3d morphable model. In *IEEE International Conference on Automatic Face and Gesture Recognition*, pages 202–207.

[Blanz and Vetter, 1999] Blanz, V. and Vetter, T. (1999). A morphable model for the synthesis of 3d faces. In *Computer Graphics, Annual Conference Series*, pages 187–194. Siggraph.

[Brand, 1999] Brand, M. (1999). Voice puppetry. In *Computer Graphics, Annual Conference Series*, pages 21–28. Siggraph.

[Brand, 2001] Brand, M. (2001). Morphable 3d models from video. In *IEEE Computer Vision and Pattern Recognition*, pages 21–28.

[Bregler et al., 1997] Bregler, C., Covell, M., and Slaney, M. (1997). Video rewrite: Driving visual speech with audio. In *Computer Graphics*, pages 353–360. Siggraph.

[Bregler and Konig, 1994] Bregler, C. and Konig, Y. (1994). Eigenlips for robust speech recognition. In *Proc. Intl. Conference on Acoustic, Speech, Signal Processing*, pages 669–672.

[Buck and et al., 2000] Buck, I. and et al. (2000). Performance-driven hand-drawn animation. In *First International Symposium on Non Photorealistic Animation and Rendering (NPAR 2000)*, pages 101–108.

[Cabral et al., 1999] Cabral, B., Olano, M., and Nemec, P. (1999). Reflection space image based rendering. In *Proc. SIGGRAPH 99*, pages 165–170.

[Campbell and Dodd, 1980] Campbell, R. and Dodd, B. (1980). Hearing by eye. *Quarterly Jounal of Experimental Psychology*, 32:85–99.

[Cascia et al., 2000] Cascia, M. L., Sclaroff, S., and Athitsos, V. (2000). Fast, reliable head tracking under varying illumination: An approach based on robust registration of texture-mapped 3d models. *IEEE Transaction on Pattern Analysis and Machine Intelligence*, 22(4):322–336.

[Chan, 1999] Chan, M. (1999). Automatic lip model extraction for constrained contour-based tracking. In *Proc. Int. Conf. of Image Processing*.

[Chellappa et al., 1995] Chellappa, R., Wilson, C., and Sirohey, S. (1995). Human and machine recognition of faces: A survey. *Proceeding of IEEE*, 83(5):705–740.

[Chen et al., 2002] Chen, H., Liang, L., Li, Y., Xu, Y., and Shum, H. (2002). Pictoon: A personalized image-based cartoon system. In *Proc. ACM Multimedia*.

[Chen and Rao, 1998] Chen, T. and Rao, R. R. (1998). Audio-visual integration in multimodal communications. *Proceedings of the IEEE*, 86(5):837–852.

[Cohen et al., 2003] Cohen, I., Sebe, N., Chen, L., Garg, A., and Huang, T. S. (2003). Facial expression recognition from video sequences: Temporal and static modeling. *Computer Vision and Image Understanding, Special Issue on Face Recognition*, 91(1-2):160–187.

[Cohen and Massaro, 1993] Cohen, M. M. and Massaro, D. W. (1993). Modeling coarticulation in synthetic visual speech. In *Models and Techniques in Compute Animations*, pages 139–156.

[Cohen-Tannoudji and et al., 1977] Cohen-Tannoudji, C. and et al. (1977). *Quantum Mechanics*. John Wiley & Sons.

[Cole et al., 1999] Cole, R., Massaro, D., de Villiers, J., Rundle, B., Shobaki, K., Wouters, J., Cohen, M., Beskow, J., Stone, P., Connors, P., Tarachow, A., and Solcher, D. (1999). New tools for interactive speech and language training: Using animated conversational agents in the classrooms of profoundly deaf children. In *Proceedings of ESCA/SOCRATES Workshop on Method and Tool Innovations for Speech Science Education*.

[Comon, 1994] Comon, P. (1994). Independent component analysis - a new concept? *Signal Processing*, 36:287–314.

[Cootes et al., 1995] Cootes, T. F., Cooper, D., Taylor, C., and Graham, J. (1995). Active shape models - their training and application. *Computer Vision and Image Understanding*, 61(1):38–59.

[Cootes et al., 1998] Cootes, T. F., Edwards, G. J., and Taylor, C. J. (1998). Active appearance models. In *European Conference on Computer Vision*, pages 484–498.

[Cosatto and Graf, 2000] Cosatto, E. and Graf, H. P. (2000). Photo-realistic talking-heads from image samples. *IEEE Trans. on Multimedia*, 2(3):152–163.

[Curinga et al., 1996] Curinga, S., Lavagetto, F., and Vignoli, F. (1996). Lip movements synthesis using time-delay neural networks. In *Proc. EUSIPCO-96*.

[Cyberware, 2003] Cyberware (2003). Cyberware. Description retrieved from http://www.cyberware.com/.

[Dariush et al., 1998] Dariush, B., Kang, S. B., and Waters, K. (1998). Spatiotemporal analysis of face profiles: Detection, segmentation, and registration. In *Proc. of the 3rd International Conference on Automatic Face and Gesture Recognition*, pages 248–253. IEEE.

[Debevec, 1998] Debevec, P. E. (1998). Rendering synthetic objects into real scenes: Bridging traditional and image-based graphics with global illumination and high dynamic range photography. In *Computer Graphics, Annual Conference Series*, pages 189–198. Siggraph.

[Debevec et al., 2000] Debevec, P. E., Hawkins, T., Tchou, C., Duiker, H.-P., Sarokin, W., and Sagar, M. (2000). Acquiring the reflectance field of a human face. In *Computer Graphics, Annual Conference Series*, pages 145–156. Siggraph.

[DeCarlo, 1998] DeCarlo, D. (1998). *Generation, Estimation and Tracking of Faces*. PhD thesis, University of Pennsylvania, Department of Computer and Information Science.

[DeCarlo and Metaxas, 2000] DeCarlo, D. and Metaxas, D. (2000). Optical flow constraints on deformable models with applications to face tracking. *International Journal of Computer Vision*, 38(2):99–127.

[DeCarlo et al., 1998] DeCarlo, D., Metaxas, D., and Stone, M. (1998). An anthropometric face model using variational techniques. In *Computer Graphics, Annual Conference Series*, pages 67–74. Siggraph.

[Dempster et al., 1977] Dempster, A., Laird, N., and Rubin, D. (1977). Maximum likelihood from incomplete data via the em algorithm. *J. Royal Stat. Soc. B*, 39:1–38.

[DiPaola, 1991] DiPaola, S. (1991). Extending the range of facial typ. . *Journal of Visualization and Computer Animation*, 2(4):129–131.

[Donato et al., 1999] Donato, G., Bartlett, M., Hager, J. C., Ekman, P., and Seinowski, T. (1999). Classifying facial actions. *IEEE Transaction on Pattern Analysis and Machine Intelligence*, 21(10):974–989.

[Eisert et al., 2000] Eisert, P., Wiegand, T., and Girod, B. (2000). Model-aided coding: A new approach to incorporate facial animation into motion-compensated video coding. *IEEE Transactions on Circuits and Systems for Video Technology*, 10(3):344–358.

[Ekman and Friesen, 1977] Ekman, P. and Friesen, W. V. (1977). *Facial Action Coding System*. Consulting Psychologists Press Inc.

[Epstein et al., 1995] Epstein, R., Hallinan, P., and Yullie, A. (1995). 5 +/- 2 eigenimages suffice: An empirical investigation of low dimensional lighting models. In *IEEE Workshop on Physics Based Vision*, pages 108–116.

[Essa and Pentland, 1997] Essa, I. and Pentland, A. (1997). Coding analysis, interpretation, and recognition of facial expressions. *IEEE Trans. on Pattern Analysis and Machine Intelligence*, pages 757–763.

[Eyetronics, 2003] Eyetronics (2003). Eyetronics. Description retrieved from http://www.eyetronics.com/.

[Ezzat et al., 2002] Ezzat, T., Geiger, G., and Poggio, T. (2002). Trainable videorealistic speech animation. In *Computer Graphics, Annual Conference Series*, pages 388–398. Siggraph.

[Ezzat and Poggio, 2000] Ezzat, T. and Poggio, T. (2000). Visual speech synthesis by morphing visemes. *International Journal of Computer Vision*, 38(1):45–57.

[FacialMuscel, 2002] FacialMuscel (2002). Facial muscel image. Retrieved from http://sfghed.ucsf.edu/ClinicImages/anatomy.htm.

[Foley and Dam, 1984] Foley, J. and Dam, A. V. (1984). *Fundamentals of interactive computer graphics*. Addison-Wesley.

[Fua and Miccio, 1998] Fua, P. and Miccio, C. (1998). From regular images to animated heads: A least squares approach. In *European Conference on Computer Vision*, pages 188–202.

[Gales and Woodland, 1996] Gales, M. and Woodland, P. (1996). Mean and variance adaptation within the mllr framework. *Computer Speech and Language*, 10:249–264.

[Georghiades et al., 1999] Georghiades, A., Belhumeur, P., and Kriegman, D. (1999). Illumination-based image synthesis: Creating novel image of human faces under diiffering pose and lighting. In *IEEE Workshop on Multi-View Modeling and Analysis of Visual Scenes*, pages 47–54.

[Georghiades et al., 2001] Georghiades, A., Belhumeur, P., and Kriegman, D. (2001). From few to many: Illumination cone models for face recognition under variable lighting and pose. *IEEE Transactions on Pattern Analysis and Machine Intelligence*, 23(6):643–660.

[Georghiades et al., 1998] Georghiades, A., Kriegman, D., and Belhumeur, P. (1998). Illumination cones for recognition under variable lighting: Faces. In *IEEE Conference on Computer Vision and Pattern Recognition*.

[Goto et al., 2001] Goto, T., Kshirsagar, S., and Magnenat-Thalmann, N. (2001). Automatic face cloning and animation. *IEEE Signal Processing Magazine*. 18(3):17–25.

[Graf et al., 2002] Graf, H., Cosatto, E., Strom, V., and Huang, F. (2002). Visual prosody: Facial movements accompanying speech. In *IEEE International Conference on Automatic Face and Gesture Recognition*.

[Greene, 1986] Greene, N. (1986). Environment mapping and other applications of world projections. *IEEE Computer Graphics and Applications*, 6(11):21–29.

[Guenter et al., 1998] Guenter, B., Grimm, C., Wood, D., Malvar, H., and Pighin, F. (1998). Making faces. In *Computer Graphics, Annual Conference Series*, pages 55–66. Siggraph.

[H26L, 2002] H26L (2002). H.26l codec reference software. Download from ftp://ftp.imtc-files.org/jvt-experts.

[Hallinan, 1994] Hallinan, P. (1994). A low-dimensional representation of human faces for arbitrary lighting conditions. In *Proc. IEEE Conference on Computer Vision and Pattern Recognition*, pages 995–999.

[Hampapur et al., 2003] Hampapur, A., Brown, L., Connell, J., Pankanti, S., Senior, A., and Tian, Y.-L. (2003). Smart surveillance: Applications, technologies and implications. In *IEEE Pacific-Rim Conference On Multimedia*.

[Hampel and et. al, 1986] Hampel, F. R. and et. al (1986). *Robust Statistics*. John Wiley & Sons.

[Hertzmann and et. al., 2001] Hertzmann, A. and et. al. (2001). Image analogies. In *Computer Graphics, Annual Conference Series*, pages 327–340. Siggraph.

[Hong et al., 2001a] Hong, P., Wen, Z., and Huang, T. S. (2001a). iface: A 3d synthetic talking face. *International Journal of Image and Graphics*, 1(1):19–26.

[Hong et al., 2001b] Hong, P., Wen, Z., and Huang, T. S. (2001b). An integrated framework for face modeling, facial motion analysis and synthesis. In *Proc. of ACM Multimedia*.

[Hong et al., 2002] Hong, P., Wen, Z., and Huang, T. S. (2002). Real-time speech driven expressive synthetic talking faces using neural networks. *IEEE Trans. on Neural Networks*, 13(4).

[H.S.Ip and Yin, 1996] H.S.Ip, H. and Yin, L. (1996). Constructing a 3d individualized head model from two orthogonal views. *The Visual Computer*, (12):254–266.

[HTK, 2004] HTK (2004). Hidden markov model toolkit (htk). Description retrieved from http://htk.eng.cam.ac.uk/.

[Hu et al., 2004] Hu, Y., Jiang, D., Yan, S., and Zhang, H. (2004). Automatic 3d reconstruction for face recognition. In *Proc. of Intl. Conf. on Automatic Face and Gesture Recognition*.

[Huang and Tao, 2001] Huang, T. and Tao, H. (2001). Visual face tracking and its application to 3d model-based video coding. In *Proc. Picture Coding Symposium*.

[IJsseldijk, 1992] IJsseldijk, F. J. (1992). Speechreading performance under different conditions of video image, repetition, and speech rate. *Journal of Speech and Hearing Research*, 35.

[Jepson et al., 2001] Jepson, A., Fleet, D., and El-Maraghi, T. (2001). Robust, on-line appearance models for vision tracking. In *IEEE Conference on Computer Vision and Pattern Recognition*, pages 415–422.

[Jolliffe, 1986] Jolliffe, I. T. (1986). *Principal Component Analysis*. Springer-Verlag.

[Kambhatla and Leen, 1997] Kambhatla, N. and Leen, T. K. (1997). Dimension reduction by local principal component analysis. *Neural Computation*, 9:1493–1516.

[Kanade et al., 2000] Kanade, T., Cohn, J., and Tian, Y. (2000). Comprehensive database for facial expression analysis. In *Prof. of IEEE Conference on Automated Face and Gesture Recognition*, pages 45–63.

[Kang and Jones, 1999] Kang, S. B. and Jones, M. (1999). Appearance-based structure from motion using linear classes of 3-d models. *Manuscript*.

[Kass et al., 1988] Kass, M., Witkin, A., and Terzopoulos, D. (1988). Snakes: Active contour models. *International Journal of Computer Vision*, 1(4):321–331.

[Kaucic and Blake, 1998] Kaucic, R. and Blake, A. (1998). Accurate, real-time, unadorned lip tracking. In *International Conference on Computer Vision*, pages 370–375.

[Kshirsagar and Magnenat-Thalmann, 2000] Kshirsagar, S. and Magnenat-Thalmann, N. (2000). Lip synchronization using linear predictive analysis. In *Proc. of IEEE Intl. Conf. on Multimedia and Expo.*, pages 1077–1080.

[Kshirsagar et al., 2001] Kshirsagar, S., Molet, T., and Magnenat-Thalmann, N. (2001). Principal components of expressive speech animation. In *Proc. of Computer Graphics International*, pages 38–44.

[Land and McCann, 1971] Land, E. and McCann, J. (1971). Lightness and retinex theory. *Journal of the Optical Society of America*, 61(1):1–11.

[Lavagetto, 1995] Lavagetto, F. (1995). Converting speech into lip movements: A multimedia telephone for hard of hearing people. In *IEEE Transactions on Rehabilitation Engineering*, pages 90–102.

[Lee and Seung, 1999] Lee, D. D. and Seung, H. S. (1999). Learning the parts of objects by non-negative matrix factorization. *Nature*, 401:788–791.

[Lee et al., 2001] Lee, K.-C., Ho, J., and Kriegman, D. (2001). Ninepoints of light: Accquiring subspaces for face recognition under variable lighting. In *IEEE Conference on Computer Vision and Pattern Recognition*, pages 357–362.

[Lee et al., 1993] Lee, Y. C., Terzopoulos, D., and Waters, K. (1993). Constructing physics-based facial models of individuals. In *Proceedings of Graphics Interface*, pages 1–8.

[Lee et al., 1995] Lee, Y. C., Terzopoulos, D., and Waters, K. (1995). Realistic modeling for facial animation. In *Computer Graphics, Annual Conference Series*, pages 55–62. SIG-GRAPH.

[Leung et al., 2000] Leung, W. H., Goudeaux, K., Panichpapiboon, S., Wang, S., and Chen, T. (2000). Networked intelligent collaborative environment (netice). In *Proc. of IEEE Intl. Conf. on Multimedia and Expo.*, pages 55–62.

[Lewis, 1989] Lewis, J. P. (1989). Algorithms for solid noise synthesis. In *Computer Graphics, Annual Conference Series*, pages 263–270. Siggraph.

[Li et al., 1993] Li, H., Roivainen, P., and Forchheimer, R. (1993). 3-d motion estimation in model-based facial image coding. *IEEE Transaction on Pattern Analysis and Machine Intelligence*, 15(6):545–555.

[Li and et al., 2001] Li, S. Z. and et al. (2001). Learning spatially localized, parts-based representation. In *IEEE Conference on Computer Vision and Pattern Recognition*.

[Liu et al., 2001a] Liu, Z., Shan, Y., and Zhang, Z. (2001a). Expressive expression mapping with ratio images. In *Computer Graphics, Annual Conference Series*, pages 271–276. Siggraph.

[Liu et al., 2001b] Liu, Z., Zhang, Z., Jacobs, C., and Cohen, M. (2001b). Rapid modeling of animated faces from video. *Journal of Visualization and Computer Animation*, 12(4):227–240.

[Lofqvist,] Lofqvist, A. Speech as audible gestures. In *Speech Production and Speech Modeling*, pages 289–322. Kluwer Academic Publishers.

[Magneneat-Thalmann et al., 1989] Magneneat-Thalmann, N., Minh, H., Angelis, M., and Thalmann, D. (1989). Design, transformation and animation of human faces. *Visual Computer*, (5):32–39.

[Marschner and Greenberg, 1997] Marschner, S. R. and Greenberg, D. P. (1997). Inverse lighting for photography. In *IST/SID Fifth Colort Imaging Conference*.

[Marschner et al., 2000] Marschner, S. R., Guenter, B., and Raghupathy, S. (2000). Modeling and rendering for realistic facial animation. In *Rendering Techniques*, pages 231–242. Springer Wien New York.

[Marschner et al., 1999] Marschner, S. R., Westin, S., Lafortune, E., Torance, K., and Greenberg, D. (1999). Image-based brdf measurement including human skin. In *Rendering Techniques*.

[Massaro, 1998] Massaro, D. (1998). *Perceiving Talking Faces*. MIT Press.

[Massaro and et al., 1999] Massaro, D. W. and et al. (1999). Picture my voice: audio to visual speech synthesis using artificial neural networks. In *Proc. AVSP 99*, pages 133–138.

[McGrath and Summerfield, 1985] McGrath, M. and Summerfield, Q. (1985). Intermodal timing relations and audiovisual speech recognition by normal-hearing adults. *Jounal of the Acoustical Society of America*, 77:678–685.

[Miller and Hoffman, 1984] Miller, G. and Hoffman, C. (1984). Illumination and reflection maps: Simulated objects in simulated and real environments. In *SIGGRAPH 84 Advanced Computer Graphics Animation Seminar Notes*. Siggraph.

[Morishima, 1998] Morishima, S. (1998). Real-time talking head driven by voice and its application to communication and entertainment. In *Proceedings of the International Conference on Auditory-Visual Speech Processing*.

[Morishima et al., 1989] Morishima, S., Aizawa, K., and Harashima, H. (1989). An intelligent facial image coding driven by speech and phoneme. In *Proc. IEEE ICASSP*, pages 1795–1798.

[Morishima and Harashima, 1991] Morishima, S. and Harashima, H. (1991). A media conversion from speech to facial image for intelligent man-machine interface. *IEEE Journal on Selected Areas in Communications*, 4:594–599.

[Morishima et al., 1998] Morishima, S., Ishikawa, T., and Terzopoulos, D. (1998). Facial muscle parameter decision from 2d frontal image. In *Proceedings of the International Conference on Pattern Recognition*, pages 160–162.

[Morishima and Yotsukura, 1999] Morishima, S. and Yotsukura, T. (1999). Face-to-face communicative avatar driven by voice. In *IEEE International Conference on Image Processing*, volume 3, pages 11–15.

[MotionAnalysis, 2002] MotionAnalysis (2002). Motion analysis corporation. Description retrived from http://www.motionanalysis.com.

[MPEG4, 1997] MPEG4 (1997). Text for cd 14496-2 video.

[Noh and Neumann, 2001] Noh, J. and Neumann, U. (2001). Expression cloning. In *Proc. SIGGRAPH 2001*, pages 277–288.

[Ostermann et al., 1998] Ostermann, J., Chen, L., , and Huang, T. S. (1998). Animated talking head with personalized 3d head model. *The Journal of VLSI Signal Processing–Systems for Signal, Image, and Video Technology*, 20(1):97–105.

[Pandey et al., 1986] Pandey, P. C., Kunov, H., and Abel, S. M. (1986). Disruptive effects of auditory signal delay on speech perception with lipreading. *Jounal of Auditory Research*, 26:27–41.

[Pandzic et al., 1999] Pandzic, I., Ostermann, J., and Millen, D. (1999). User evaluation: Synthetic talking faces for interactive services. *The Visual Computer*, 15:330–340.

[Parke, 1972] Parke, F. I. (1972). Computer generated animation of faces. In *ACM National Conference*.

[Parke, 1974] Parke, F. I. (1974). *A Parametric Model of human Faces*. PhD thesis, University of Utah.

[Parke and Waters, 1996] Parke, F. I. and Waters, K. (1996). *Computer Facial Animation*. AKPeters, Wellesley, Massachusetts.

[Pelachaud et al., 1991] Pelachaud, C., Badler, N. I., and Steedman, M. (1991). Linguistic issues in fcial animation. In *Computer Animation*, pages 15–30.

[Phillips et al., 2000] Phillips, P. J., Moon, H., Rizvi, S. A., and Rauss, P. J. (2000). The feret evaluation methodology for face-recognition algorithms. *IEEE Transactions on Pattern Analysis and Machine Intelligence*, 22(10):1090–1104.

[Pighin et al., 1998] Pighin, F., Hecker, J., Lischinski, D., Szeliski, R., and Salesin, D. H. (1998). Synthesizing realistic facial expressions from photographs. In *Proc. SIGGRAPH 98*, pages 75–84.

[Pighin et al., 1999] Pighin, F., Salesin, D. H., and Szeliski, R. (1999). Resynthesizing facial animation through 3d model-based tracking. In *International Conference on Computer Vision*, pages 143–150.

[Platt and Badler, 1981] Platt, S. and Badler, N. (1981). Animating facial expression. *Computer Graphics*, 15(3):245–252.

[Rabiner, 1989] Rabiner, L. (1989). A tutorial on hidden markov models and selected applications in speech recognition. *Proc. IEEE*, 77(2):257–286.

[Rabiner and Juang, 1993] Rabiner, L. and Juang, B. H. (1993). *Fundamentals of Speech Recognition*. Prentice Hall.

[Rabiner and Shafer, 1978] Rabiner, L. R. and Shafer, R. W. (1978). *Digital Processing of Speech Signal*. Prentice Hall.

[Ramamoorthi, 2002] Ramamoorthi, R. (2002). Analytic pca construction for theoretical analysis of lighting variability in images of a lambertian object. *IEEE Trans. on Pattern Analysis and Machine Intelligence*, 24(10).

[Ramamoorthi and Hanrahan, 2001a] Ramamoorthi, R. and Hanrahan, P. (2001a). An efficient representation for irradiance environment maps. In *Computer Graphics, Annual Conference Series*, pages 497–500. Siggraph.

[Ramamoorthi and Hanrahan, 2001b] Ramamoorthi, R. and Hanrahan, P. (2001b). A signal-processing framework for inverse rendering. In *Computer Graphics, Annual Conference Series*, pages 117–128. Siggraph.

[Rao and Chen, 1996] Rao, R. and Chen, T. (1996). Exploiting audio-visual correlation in coding of talking head sequences. In *Picture Coding Symposium*.

[Reveret and Essa, 2001] Reveret, L. and Essa, I. (2001). Visual coding and tracking of speech related facial motion. In *Proc. of Workshop on Cues in Communication*.

[Riklin-Raviv and Shashua, 1999] Riklin-Raviv, T. and Shashua, A. (1999). The quotient image: Class based re-rendering and recongnition with varying illuminations. In *IEEE Conference on Computer Vision and Pattern Recognition*, pages 566–571.

[Romdhani and Vetter, 2003] Romdhani, S. and Vetter, T. (2003). Efficient, robust and accurate fitting of a 3d morphable model. In *IEEE International conference on Computer Vision*, pages 59–66.

[Shi and Tomasi, 1994] Shi, J. and Tomasi, C. (1994). Good features to track. In *IEEE Conference on Computer Vision and Pattern Recognition*, pages 593–600.

[Sim and Kanade, 2001] Sim, T. and Kanade, T. (2001). Combining models and exemplars for face recognition: An illuminating example. In *Proc. of Workshop on Models versus Exemplars in Computer Vision*.

[SphericalHarmonic, 2002] SphericalHarmonic (2002). Spharmonickit. Description retrived from http://www.cs.dartmouth.edu/~geelong/sphere/.

[Stork and Hennecke, 1996] Stork, D. G. and Hennecke, M. E., editors (1996). *Speechreading by Humans and Machines: Models, Systems and Applications*. Springer.

[Stoschek, 2000] Stoschek, A. (2000). Image-based re-rendering of faces for continuous pose and illumination directions. In *IEEE Conference on Computer Vision and Pattern Recognition*, pages 582–587.

[Tao, 1999] Tao, H. (1999). *Non-Rigid Motion Modeling And Analysis In Video Sequence For Realistic Facial Animation*. PhD thesis, University of Illinois at Urbana-Champaign, Department of Electrical and Computer Engineering.

[Tao and Huang, 1999] Tao, H. and Huang, T. S. (1999). Explanation-based facial motion tracking using a piecewise bezier volume deformation model. In *IEEE Conference on Computer Vision and Pattern Recognition*.

[Terzopoulos and Waters, 1990a] Terzopoulos, D. and Waters, K. (1990a). Analysis of dynamic facial images using physical and anatomical models. In *International Conference on Computer Vision*, pages 727–732.

[Terzopoulos and Waters, 1990b] Terzopoulos, D. and Waters, K. (1990b). Physically-based facial modeling and animation. *Journal of Visualization and Computer Animation*, 1(4):73–80.

[Tian and Bolle, 2001] Tian, Y. and Bolle, R. M. (2001). Automatic neutral face detection using location and shape features. Computer Science Research Report RC 22259, IBM Research.

[Tian et al., 2002] Tian, Y., Kanade, T., and Cohn, J. (2002). Evaluation of gabor-wavelet-based facial action unit recognition in image sequences of increasing complexity. In *Prof. of IEEE Conference on Automated Face and Gesture Recognition*.

[Todd et al., 1980] Todd, J. T., Leonard, S. M., Shaw, R. E., and Pittenger, J. B. (1980). The perception of human growth. *Scientific American*, (1242):106–114.

[Toyama and Blake, 2002] Toyama, K. and Blake, A. (2002). Probabilistic tracking with exemplar in a metric space. *International Journal of Computer Vision*, 48(1):9–19.

[Tu et al., 2003] Tu, J., Wen, Z., Tao, H., , and Huang, T. S. (2003). Exploiting audio-visual correlation in coding of talking head sequences. In *Picture Coding Symposium*.

[Turk and Pentland, 1991] Turk, M. and Pentland, A. (1991). Eigenfaces for recognition. *Journal of Cognitive Neuroscience*, 3(1):71–96.

[Vacchetti et al., 2003] Vacchetti, L., Lepetit, V., and Fua, P. (2003). Stable 3-d tracking in real-time using integrated context information. In *IEEE Conference on Computer Vision and Pattern Recognition*.

[Vetter and Poggio, 1997] Vetter, T. and Poggio, T. (1997). Linear object classes and image synthesis from a single example image. *IEEE Transations on Pattern Analysis and Machine Intelligence*, 19(7):733–742.

[Vignoli et al., 1996] Vignoli, F., Curinga, S., and Lavagetto, F. (1996). A neural clustering architecture for estimating visible articulatory trajectories. In *International Conference on Artificial Neural Networks*, pages 863–869.

[Wachtman et al., 2001] Wachtman, G., Cohn, J., , VanSwearingen, J., and Manders, E. (2001). Automated tracking of facial features in facial neuromotor disorders. *Plastic and Reconstructive Surgery*, 107:1124–1133.

[Wahba, 1990] Wahba, G. (1990). Splines models for observational data. *Series in Applied Mathematics*, 59.

[Waters, 1987] Waters, K. (1987). A muscle model for animating three-dimensional facial expression. *Computer Graphics*, 22(4):17–24.

[Waters and Levergood, 1993] Waters, K. and Levergood, T. M. (1993). Decface, an automatic lip-synchronization algorithm for synthetic faces. Technical Report CRL 93-4, Cambridge Research Lab.

[Waters et al., 1996] Waters, K., Rehg, J. M., Loughlin, M., and et al (1996). Visual sensing of humans for active public interfaces. Technical Report CRL 96-5, Cambridge Research Lab.

[Wen et al., 2001] Wen, Z., Hong, P., and Huang, T. S. (2001). Real time speech driven facial animation using formant analysis. In *Proc. of IEEE Intl. Conf. on Multimedia and Expo*.

[Wen and Huang, 2003] Wen, Z. and Huang, T. S. (2003). Capturing subtle facial motions in 3d face tracking. In *IEEE Conference on Computer Vision*, volume 2, pages 1343–1350.

[Wen and Huang, 2004] Wen, Z. and Huang, T. S. (2004). Hybrid face analysis videos. Description retrived from http://www.ifp.uiuc.edu/~zhenwen/publication.htm.

[Wen et al., 2003] Wen, Z., Liu, Z., and Huang, T. S. (2003). Face relighting with radiance environment maps. In *IEEE Conference on Computer Vision and Pattern Recognition*, volume 2, pages 158–165.

[Williams et al., 1997] Williams, J. J., Rutledge, J. C., Garstecki, D. C., and Katsaggelos, A. K. (1997). Frame rate and viseme analysis for multimedia applications. In *IEEE Workshop on Multimedia Signal Processing*, volume 2, pages 13–18.

[Williams, 1990] Williams, L. (1990). Performace-driven facial animation. In *Computer Graphics*, pages 235–242. Siggraph.

[Woodland, 1999] Woodland, P. (1999). Speaker adaptation: Techniques and challenges. In *International Workshop on Automatic Speech Recognition and Understanding*.

[Yu et al., 1999] Yu, Y., Debevec, P. E., Malik, J., and Hawkins, T. (1999). Inverse global illumination: Recovering reflectance models of real scenes from photogrpahs. In *Computer Graphics, Annual Conference Series*, pages 215–224. Siggraph.

[Yullie et al., 1992] Yullie, A., Hallinan, P., and Cohen, D. (1992). Feature extraction from faces using deformable templates. *International Journal of Computer Vision*, 8(2):99–111.

[Zhang et al., 2001] Zhang, L., Dugas-Phocion, G., Samson, J.-S., and Seitz, S. M. (2001). Single view modeling of free-form scenes. In *IEEE Conference on Computer Vision and Pattern Recognition*, pages 1990–1997.

[Zhang and Samaras, 2003] Zhang, L. and Samaras, D. (2003). Face recognition under variable lighting using harmonic image exemplars. In *IEEE Conference on Computer Recognition and Pattern Recognition*, volume 1, pages 19–25.

[Zhang et al., 2003] Zhang, Q., Liu, Z., Guo, B., and Shum, H. (2003). Geometry-driven photorealistic facial expression synthesis. In *Symposium on Computer Animation*.

[Zhang et al., 2000] Zhang, Y., Levinson, S., and Huang, T. (2000). Speaker independent audio-visual speech recognition. In *Proc. of IEEE Intl. Conf. on Multimedia and Expo.*, pages 1073–1076.

[Zhang et al., 1998] Zhang, Z., Lyons, M., Schuster, M., and Akamatsu, S. (1998). Comparison between geometric-based and gabor-wavelets-based facial expression recognition using multi-layer perceptron. In *Proc. of International Conference on Automatic Face and Gesture Recognition*, pages 454–459.

[Zhao and R.Chellappa, 2000] Zhao, W. and R.Chellappa (2000). Illumination-insensitive face recognition using symmetric shape-from-shading. In *IEEE Conference on Computer Recognition and Pattern Recognition*, pages 286–293.

[Zhao et al., 2000] Zhao, W., R.Chellappa, and Rosenfeld, A. (2000). Face recognition: A literature survey. Technical Report CAR-TR-948, University of Maryland at College Park, Center for Automation Research.

[Zheng, 1994] Zheng, J. Y. (1994). Acquiring 3-d models from sequences of contours. *IEEE Transactions on Pattern Analysis and Machine Intelligence*, 16(2):163–178.

Index